In Amma's Splendor

by

by Swami Ramakrishnananda Puri

Mata Amritanandamayi Center
San Ramon, California, USA

In Amma's Splendor
By Swami Ramakrishnananda Puri

Published By:
Mata Amritanandamayi Center
P.O. Box 613
San Ramon, CA 94583
United States

First edition September 2025, 1000 copies

In India: www.amritapuri.org

International: www.amma.org

Contents

Preface

Once Amma was asked how she is able to feel compassion for everyone she meets. She answered simply, "Amma cannot be otherwise. The feeling of oneness is very real to me. A cow may be black, brown, or red, but its milk is always white." Just as the milk from every cow is alike, the Self in all is one, not many. It only appears divided to those who mistakenly see themselves as separate.

Amma is striving to uplift all of us, so we may come to see the world as she does. She does this not by preaching, but by example, by embodying that vision of Oneness in every moment. With infinite patience, Amma is helping us to see the world through her eyes. And slowly but surely, she is succeeding. As we walk along life's path, all we need to do is hold on to Amma's little finger. If we can do that, we will begin to see as she sees, with a vision rooted in love and unity. And the infinite divine qualities of Amma described in these pages, the very glories Krishna speaks of in Chapter 10 of the *Bhagavad Gita*, will begin to shine through our thoughts, our words, and our lives.

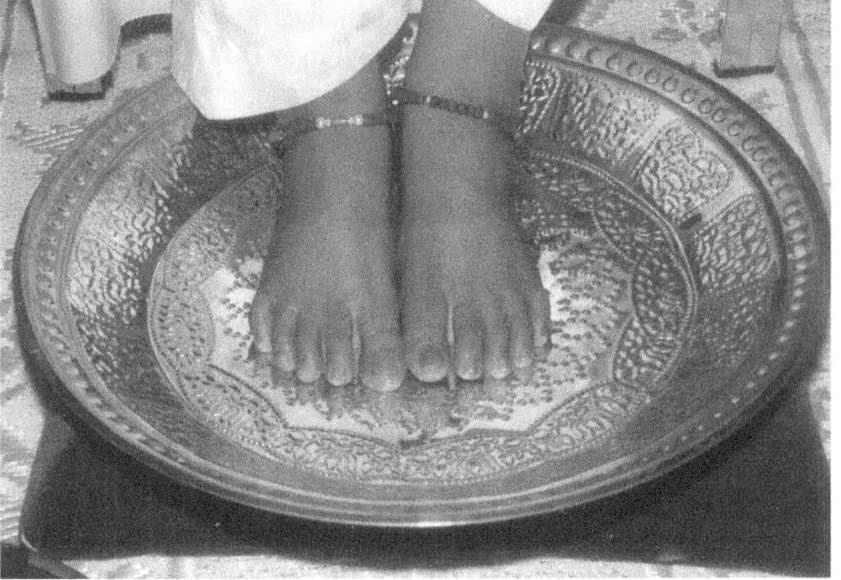

Offered at the Lotus Feet
of My Beloved Sadguru,
Sri Mata Amritanandamayi Devi

Part 1: Knowledge of the Self

1—The Real Birthday

There is a popular saying: "You can fool some of the people all of the time. You can fool all of the people some of the time, but you cannot fool all of the people all of the time." But I like to use a different version: "You can fool some of the people all of the time. You can fool all of the people some of the time. But don't worry about the rest—they'll fool themselves." This may make us laugh, but according to great spiritual masters like Amma, we all belong to the third category. We are fooling ourselves.

How do we do this? By completely misunderstanding who and what we really are. We think we are the body. We think we are the mind. We think we are the intellect. We think we are everything other than what we truly are, pure consciousness. Somehow, we mistake ourselves for what we are not, while denying what we truly are. The funny thing is, no one has done this to us. We do it to ourselves.

We are like children struggling to untie their knotted-up shoelaces. Someone else, like our mother or father, has to come and help. This is how it is with us and our guru. Our minds have become tangled in confusion, and it is our guru's job to come and help us untie these knots.

A famous story in the scriptures called "The Tenth Man" illustrates this perfectly... Long ago, ten people went on a pilgrimage together. At one point, they came to a river they had to cross, and the waters were quite rough. Once they made it to the other side, the leader decided to count heads. He wanted to make sure everyone had safely crossed without drowning, but each time he counted the pilgrims, there were only nine of them. Panic set in. He counted again; still there were only nine.

But fate was kind. A wise, elderly traveler stepped forward to help. He immediately understood the problem and asked the leader to count everyone again. The leader carefully counted each pilgrim before him, then muttered hopelessly, "Nine... only nine."

The traveler laughed compassionately. "My dear foolish brother, you haven't counted yourself. *You* are the tenth man!"

In this story, the wise traveler represents the guru, the one who helps us emerge from confusion. With quiet grace, the guru reveals what we had overlooked, what was always here: our true nature.

We are all acting like the tenth man. The time has come to analyze our situation and understand what the problem is, so we can set it right. By now many of us have a clear understanding of spirituality and its core teaching that we are the Self. This raises an interesting question. If we are pure consciousness, then why aren't we free?

I would say the problem is that we don't really *believe* we are pure consciousness. Let me share a brief story to illustrate this.

Once a guru asked one of his disciples, "Who are you?"

The disciple confidently responded, "I am the *Atma*—the pure consciousness beyond body, mind, and intellect."

The guru smiled and asked, "How long will it take you to attain liberation?"

In a fraction of a second, the disciple's confidence vanished, and he muttered, "Oh, I don't know... Maybe, with your grace, at the moment of death."

The guru retorted, "If you are the Atma, how can you doubt it?"

The disciple replied, "I know the Atma is birthless, but I don't know if *I* am birthless."

And that is the problem! Even though we understand what the Atma is, we don't really believe that the Atma is our own essence. We continue to believe we are the body, mind, and intellect.

Amma's knowledge, on the other hand, is perfect. She has no doubt about who she is. We, however, suffer because we've forgotten who we are. To unravel this confusion, we must begin to see clearly, like Amma does. If we can do this, we will realize we were never the limited being we imagined. We will see that we were never born, and we will never die.

This reminds me of an incident that took place about thirty years ago, just after I joined the ashram... Amma's birthday was approaching, so a few of us *brahmacharis* went to Amma with plans for a big celebration. Amma's words surprised us all. "I was never born," she said, "so how can I have a birthday?"

As we had all just begun spiritual life, we didn't understand what Amma was saying. We thought she was just trying to avoid unnecessary expenses. But Amma was doing so much more. She was trying to teach us about her true nature and our own.

Actually, every time Amma's birthday rolls around, she inevitably says, "The real birthday is the day you realize you were never born, and you will never die." And so, rather than a personal celebration, Amma's birthday has become an opportunity to launch new charitable projects and to lead hundreds of thousands of her children in a sincere, heartfelt prayer for world peace.

2—Know Your Level

A devotee once shared an experience with me. He had just met Amma and was head over heels, overwhelmed with devotion. He felt like he had hit the spiritual jackpot. After meeting Amma, everything started going well in his life. He was happier and more prosperous than ever. When he was at Amma's programs, he felt carried away by a joy he couldn't explain.

Later that year on U.S. Tour, during Guru Purnima, he chose a bright yellow garland to place around Amma's neck. As he joined the *darshan* line, he thought about how lucky he was to be Amma's devotee. His only wish was to silently express his deep gratitude while garlanding Amma.

Here is what he said to me when he reflected back on that evening: "Swami ji, despite my feelings of gratitude back then, I now see that I was actually full of ego and pride. In fact, I felt that my feelings of gratitude were somehow a reflection of *my* glory. And even though I was approaching Amma with the right attitude, I felt egoistic about feeling gratitude in the first place... Then something terrible happened. As I got closer to Amma, my mind started insulting her. Each time I thought, 'Amma, thank you so much for being my guru,' my mind chimed in with insulting names to call her."

"I was like the bald king in Amma's story who is given a hair-growing tonic that will only work if he does *not* think of rats. Just as the king couldn't stop thinking of rats, I couldn't stop thinking of insults. I suddenly realized how little control I had over my mind... how far I still had to go on the spiritual path. I was so humbled. So, I did the only thing I could think of: I started chanting my mantra as intensely as I could. Otherwise, I might have mentally insulted Amma during my darshan."

After hearing his story, I replied, "That was Amma's Guru Purnima *prasad* for you. She wanted to show you your limitations.

We can't begin to grow spiritually until we face what's really going on inside and accept where we are on the path."

When we first come to Amma, most of us have very little control over our minds. We're filled with negativities, but for the most part, we're unaware of them. And though we may experience bliss in Amma's presence, she also reveals the darkness within us. That can be painful, but it's essential to know where we truly are on the path, so we can evolve.

Facing what lies beneath the surface takes courage. But without that courage, we can't grow stronger. As Amma consistently reminds us, we're not helpless kittens. We are lion cubs learning to roar.

3—Ready to Face Anything

To become truly fearless, we must face what many shy away from: the nature of life, death, and that which never changes. In the *Phaedo*, one of Plato's most famous philosophical works, Socrates is arrested on false charges and sentenced to death. The *Phaedo* recounts the final hours of Socrates' life, where he famously says, "Those who practice philosophy in the right way are training to die... and they fear death least of all men."

The exact same idea is expressed in India's ancient *Taittiriya Upanishad*, which says: *vidvān na vibhedati kutaścana* — "The one endowed with Self-knowledge is not afraid of anything" (2.4). So, whether we are looking from the Western perspective or the ancient Indian perspective, both urge us to overcome the fear of death.

As the following story makes clear, Amma, like the great souls who came before her, embodies fearlessness. In 2016, a government official visited the ashram, and it was my job to take him on a tour of the grounds and then introduce him to Amma. He was a religious person and quite learned in some of India's scriptures, particularly the *Vastu Shastra*, which lays out the ancient Indian science of architecture. Like *feng shui*, the *Vastu Shastra* teaches us how to build our homes and arrange the kitchen, altar, and other rooms to harness Mother Nature's positive energies.

As this officer spoke with Amma, he pointed out several things in the ashram that were out of tune with vastu. He told Amma that if these things were corrected, it would greatly benefit the community.

Amma listened, half nodding her head. But to be honest, she didn't seem very interested in what he was saying. The officer noticed and asked, "Amma, don't you have faith in vastu?"

"Son, of course I do," Amma replied. "All of the sciences in the scriptures are based on the visions of the ancient sages. As such, they are all based in truth. The sages would never share pointless knowledge. For people obsessed with success, wealth, and perfect results, *Vastu Shastra* and astrology can be very helpful. As for me, I am always ready to face anything. So, I don't concern myself with these things very much."

Listening to Amma speak that day, I thought, 'Actually, Ready-to-Face-Anything should be Amma's middle name. We should rename her Shri Mata Ready-to-Face-Anything Amritanandamayi Devi.'

No matter how large the darshan crowd, Amma is ready to face it. No matter how demanding the tour schedule, Amma is ready to face it. No matter how vast the destruction caused by a natural disaster, Amma is ready to face it. And perhaps most remarkably, no matter how mired in spiritual ignorance her disciples and devotees may be, Amma is ready to face it. Like Socrates in the *Phaedo*, Amma fears neither death nor anything else.

What is the source of Amma's fearlessness? It's her knowledge of who she is. She knows she is the Atma; she knows she is the True Self – infinite, eternal, blissful consciousness. She has zero confusion about this. As a result, Amma knows she can never be harmed in any way.

The True Self is ever detached from everything; it remains ever apart. The great *Vedanta* philosopher Adi Shankaracharya put it this way: "The mirage waters can never muddy the desert sands." Just as the desert stays dry and untouched beneath the mirage of water, the True Self remains pure and unharmed despite the false appearances and challenges of the world. This understanding is the source of Amma's fearlessness.

As for us, we misunderstand who we are. We mistakenly think we are our body, mind, and senses and fail to understand our intrinsic nature. This leads to a sense of separation and fear.

Once a guru was sitting with a few of his disciples and posed this riddle to them: "A truck driver was going the wrong way down a one-way street as fast as he could. On the way, he passed right by a traffic cop, but the policeman didn't give him a ticket. Why?"

The disciples were stumped. None of them could come up with the right answer. Just then, the cook returned from his *seva* preparing the evening meal. The guru turned to him and asked the same question.

"That's easy," the disciple responded. "It's because the truck driver was not driving. He was walking."

The guru smiled and said to the others, "You couldn't find the answer because you saw the man only as a truck driver, not as a human being. This happens all the time. We confuse someone's role with who they really are. But spiritual life is about learning to see the essence, so we're not fooled by appearances."

Amma says we all misperceive reality in the same way, and that we must learn to look beyond the surface, to the center, to the heart. Only then will we begin to understand and live in the awareness that we are not the body, the mind, or the intellect. Only then will we recognize ourselves as the substratum of all.

When this realization dawns, we will easily remain calm in all situations, just like Amma. If you watch her carefully, you will see that Amma is never disturbed, no matter how intense the situation. This is because she knows who she truly is. She knows she is not the body that can be harmed. When we develop this same understanding, we too will be able to remain perfectly at ease no matter what life throws at us. But as long as we identify with the superficial aspects of ourselves, aspects that are easily shaken by the changing world, how can we *not* be disturbed?

From the beginning, Amma faced many obstacles. The ashram was surrounded by a largely uneducated village with many staunch atheists. On top of that, Amma had to overcome gender discrimination, caste prejudice, and countless other challenges. But no matter how difficult these situations were, Amma always remained tranquil and fearless. Once I asked Amma, "Have you ever felt disturbed? Ever?"

Amma thought for a moment and replied, "No, never. For me it is simply impossible." And yet, although Amma is never disturbed by anything, she *is* concerned—concerned about her children's welfare.

All of us want to be peaceful and fearless like Amma. No one wants to feel tense and afraid all the time. And so, we look to Amma and pray that one day we can also be like her. But, at the same time, we must do our part. We must introspect to know where we are on the path. Actually, this is true in any sphere of life. A student who doesn't know basic algebra cannot jump into a trigonometry class. A student who hasn't taken pre-med classes cannot start diagnosing patients. It is the same in spiritual life.

Advanced spiritual masters like Amma shine before us like a pole star, guiding us forward. But those of us in the spiritual trenches have to be honest with ourselves about where we are, what our level of spiritual understanding is, and what our capabilities are.

A few years ago, Amma was talking with someone who was experiencing many personal problems. Several people he cared about were spreading lies about him. One had even leveled a lawsuit against him. Amma explained that during certain astrological periods in life, no matter what we do, our words and actions will be taken the wrong way.

The man replied, "Amma, that is exactly what is happening to me."

Amma suggested that he do as many good deeds as possible during this rough patch. She continued, "Son, even these good deeds may be taken the wrong way, but they will lessen the effects of your past bad actions. Eventually you will come out of it."

The man nodded and said, "I understand, Amma. From now on, I will share as much selfless love as I can."

"Yes, son," Amma replied.

"So, Amma, you are saying the best defense is no defense at all. Right?"

"No," Amma replied. "It's not like that... I can follow that path because I can accept anything that comes in life. You are not at that level. For now, you must stand up for yourself and deal with the situations that arise."

Most of us are like this fellow. We are not ready to accept everything that comes. This is why Amma advises most people to try to change the external situation they are facing. Because she understands our level, she often advises us to work for better things for ourselves and our families, to sincerely contribute to society, and to confront unrighteousness when we see it.

But if the things we are striving for don't work out, we should do our best to be like Amma and inwardly accept what comes. This is why it is so important to cultivate an inner attitude of surrender and acceptance. This is the first step for those of us who still have desires in the world. In a nutshell Amma is saying, "Try your best, and accept the rest." Nurturing this attitude opens us up to inner peace and spiritual progress. If we stay true to this path, it will eventually take us to total acceptance and fearlessness.

But the path of acceptance can be challenging. Let's return to Amma's conversation with the vastu expert to explore this. A few days later, a man who had heard the entire conversation asked me, "Swamiji, I understand that Amma can face anything, but she is running an institution with schools, hospitals, and many humanitarian projects. On a practical level, wouldn't it be best if the ashram and all its projects adhered to the principles of vastu and astrology?"

I replied, "Amma is a *mahatma*. By her mere resolve, she can have everything go perfectly, without following the rules of vastu or astrology. The ashram, Embracing the World, the Mata Amritanandamayi Math—none of these are for Amma's benefit. They are all for the benefit of the world, not just for the poor and sick who are being helped, but also for the disciples and devotees who are volunteering their time on these projects."

Even though Amma's sevites may not yet be ready for everything life brings, Amma wants to raise them to that level. She wants all of them to meet challenges with courage and grace, just like her, and the only way she can do that is by making the road bumpy from time to time. She places sharp turns, potholes, and obstacles along the way because it is through these challenges that growth unfolds.

Amma's job as a spiritual master is very tricky; it requires delicate balance. The path has to blend just the right amount of chaos with just the right amount of smoothness. Amma doesn't want the path to be totally chaotic because then nothing will get done. But at the same time, Amma doesn't want things to be totally organized either. If the ride is too smooth, no one will grow. So, Amma chooses to balance the two. It is only in the balance of chaos and organization that Amma can accomplish two important goals at once: successful humanitarian projects that uplift the world and the molding of disciples and devotees who are ready for anything.

Ultimately, Amma's goal is to turn us all into little Ammas. But how is this possible? The death of Socrates, described by Plato, provides a wonderful answer... "As the time to drink the Hemlock drew near, Socrates teased his disciples for their misplaced fear, saying, 'You seem to have a childish fear that the wind will dissolve and scatter my soul as it leaves this body, especially if I happen to die in a high wind and not in calm weather.'"

Socrates' light-heartedness in the face of death dispelled his students' dark mood. Laughing, one of them replied, "Assuming that we are afraid, Socrates, try to change our minds. Or, rather, do not assume that we are afraid, perhaps there is a child in us who has these fears. So, try to persuade that child not to fear death like a boogeyman."

Socrates replied, "You should sing a charm over the fear-filled child every day until you have charmed away his fears."

Our Upanishads celebrate the same fearlessness: *vidvān na vibhedati kutaścana* (*The one endowed with Self-knowledge is not afraid of anything*). In the end, Self-knowledge is the answer to the riddle of death.

For that knowledge to become firm, three spiritual practices are needed: *sravanam, mananam,* and *nididhyasanam*. Stage one is sravanam—listening to an enlightened soul like Amma explain the truth of our real nature. Stage two is mananam—deeply reflecting on her teachings and overcoming all doubts. And stage three is nididhyasanam—mentally affirming her teachings over and over. This threefold practice brings us under the sway of "Amma's charm," a state in which we know, through and through, that there is no such thing as death.

A few years back someone asked Amma how her love was different from ours. Amma replied, "The only difference is that my love has no strings attached. Parents bring up their children with love, but that love is always mixed with expectations. For example, parents may expect their children to look after them in old age. There is nothing wrong with that, but I don't have such expectations of anyone." In essence Amma was saying she is ready for anything and accepts everyone and everything as they are, no matter what.

But the conversation didn't end there. Amma continued, "For me, there is no such thing as death. I just live in the present. When death doesn't exist, how can I fear it? Other people think about the future and worry about it. As a child grows up, expectations arise. The parents expect their children to take care of them... But I live on my own. I am totally Self-dependent."

For someone like Amma, who understands that time and space arise in her, are sustained by her, and then merge back into her, death is a fairy tale. When this is the case, there is no scope for worry. This is the charm, the wise song, Socrates is referring to—that "in truth, death does not exist." And no one sings that charm better than Amma.

On his deathbed, Socrates tells his disciples that nothing in the entire world is more valuable than the charm-singer, the enlightened one. In fact, moments before his death Socrates says to his disciples, "You should search for such a charmer, sparing neither trouble nor expense, for there is nothing on which you could spend your time to greater advantage."

This sentiment has always been part of the Indian tradition. The *Guru Gita* says:

na guroradhikam tattvam na guroradhikam tapah |
tattva-jñanat-param nāsti tasmai sri-guruve namah||

There is no reality higher than the guru. There is no austerity higher than devotion to the guru. There is no truth superior to the guru's knowledge. Thus, to the guru, I offer my prostration.

We are all so fortunate to have found Amma—Amma who is the best of charm-singers, who is ready for anything, whose love calls us beyond the fear of death.

4—Avoiding Action Is Not Liberation

When she is in India, Amma stays in a small apartment. It has two rooms: a small bedroom and a main room, where she receives guests and holds meetings. She shares this apartment with an attendant, Swamini Srilakshmi Prana, and Shakti, the dog. Swamini Krishnamrita Prana lives just upstairs. When Amma goes on tour to embrace thousands around the world, three or four ashram ladies always come to stay in the apartment. Amma insists on this because she doesn't see the apartment as hers and does not want the space to be left unused.

Everyone who stays in Amma's room says it feels incredibly peaceful. In fact, the ladies who stay there are convinced they are not alone in the apartment, that there are subtle beings enjoying the good energy too. Sometimes, they say, Amma's veena suddenly strums all on its own, and often things they know they put in one place suddenly appear somewhere else. When they stay there, they all have intense, profound dreams.

Once, while Amma was away on her 2016 Indian Tour, a girl staying in Amma's room dreamt that Amma appeared, walked over to her, and said, "While I am gone, I need you to give darshan in my place." With that, she walked through the door.

The very next minute the girl was face-to-face with a huge crowd of people all wanting darshan. Many of them cried as they shared their problems with her. At times, the crowd squeezed in so tightly that she could barely breathe. Despite all this, the girl tried her best and kept giving darshan. She genuinely wanted to help. At the same time, she was confused, uncomfortable, and hoping that Amma would come back quickly. Worst of all, she found herself getting irritated with those who came for darshan and found herself snapping at them. Then she would remember, "Wait, I am sitting in Amma's chair! I can't act like this." When she finally woke up, she was completely exhausted.

As this dream shows, Amma's job is not easy. It is physically and mentally exhausting. Actually, darshan is never just a 9-to-5 job for Amma. It is more like a 24/7 job with no weekends or holidays off. In fact, the weekends are when the big crowds come to see Amma.

Despite Amma's tremendous activity during darshan, she remains completely peaceful, relaxed, and serene. In fact, seeing Amma's tranquility in the midst of action is what led many of us to believe in liberation in the first place. Her darshan is proof that *liberation does not mean running away from action*. It means staying connected with the source of bliss while we act.

Most people in the world lack this perspective. For them, work means anxiety; it is something to escape at all costs. When their jobs create too much stress, such people find all kinds of ways to escape: from sick days to vacations, from jury duty to resignation letters.

This reminds me of a joke.

Once, while two factory workers were chatting during their coffee break, one said to the other, "I bet I can make the boss give me the rest of the day off."

"Hmmm...I'm not so sure," said the other man. "He's pretty strict."

"Just watch," his friend replied.

With that, he did a backward flip and hung himself upside down from a ceiling beam.

"Hey you! What are you doing up there?" the boss shouted to the hanging man.

"Hi, boss," the man replied in a friendly tone. "I'm a light bulb today."

"My God!" the boss said. "You've been working so hard you've gone crazy. Take the day off!"

Seeing his co-worker get a free vacation day, the other man made his way towards the door and shouted, "Boss, I'm taking the day off too!"

"You're not going anywhere," snapped the boss. "Get back here!"

"What?" the man replied. "With the light bulb gone do you really expect me to work in the dark?"

Most of us are like these two fellows. We think that work is to blame for the tension in our lives, and we try to escape it. When that doesn't work, we often just barrel through and deal with the stress as best we can.

But Amma is living proof that there is a much better way. If escaping work was the way to peace, then Amma would never be peaceful. She never takes a day off. Every single day, Amma either gives darshan or works on her humanitarian projects. More often than not she does both at the same time. During those rare moments when Amma does have free time, she reads the huge pile of letters she receives every day from devotees all over the world. Amma's attendant, Swamini Srilakshmi, once told me that Amma even reads letters while brushing her teeth!

Amma's peace and bliss do not come from sidestepping work; they come from constant awareness of her real nature. Her secret is that no matter how active she is on the outside, she remains ever actionless within, steeped in the knowledge that, "It is the body alone that is acting. I, the pure consciousness, am doing nothing at all."

Krishna expresses the same truth in the *Bhagavad Gita* when he speaks these words:

naiva kiñcitkaromīti yukto manyeta tattvavit |
paśyan śṛṇvanspṛśañjighrannaśnangacchansvapan śvasan ||
pralapanvisṛjangṛhṇannunmiṣannimiṣannapi |
indriyāṇīndriyārtheṣu vartanta iti dhārayan ||

Even while seeing, hearing, touching, smelling, eating, moving, sleeping, breathing, speaking, evacuating, holding, opening and closing the eyes, the knower of reality, who is rooted in that truth, should think, I do nothing at all, remembering that it is the senses that reside in the sense objects. (5.8–9)

The actionless action Lord Krishna refers to here is the way to liberation. It's important to note that liberation does not dawn when we stop performing actions; it dawns when we stop identifying ourselves as the *doer* of actions. Simply put, liberation is about identifying with the deepest, truest aspect of ourselves, the part that is never affected by the experiences of the body and the mind.

This reminds me of another joke. Once a man was taken to court for kicking another man. After hearing the plaintiff's side of the case, the judge asked the defendant, "Why did you do it? Why did you kick him?"

The man answered, "I didn't do it. My leg did."

The judge looked down at the man and said, smiling, "Okay, wise guy. Then, we will put your leg in jail with or without you!"

But the defendant was a step ahead of the judge. He stood up, unscrewed his fake leg, and handed it over to the bailiff.

Please don't take this joke the wrong way. It is just a joke meant to show that mahatmas know that they are neither the performer of actions nor the enjoyer of the results. They are the ever-peaceful witness who can take life as a *leela*, a playful game.

And unlike the man in the joke, a mahatma would never do anything to harm anyone. It's impossible, for mahatmas see themselves as one with all creatures. They always put themselves in others' shoes before speaking or acting. Krishna himself clearly says this in the *Bhagavad Gita*:

ātmā upamyena sarvatra samam pasyati yo'rjuna |
sukham va yadi va duhkham sa yogi paramo matah || (6.32)

O Arjuna, one who views others' happiness and sorrow
as his own, that yogi is considered supreme.

If we can cultivate the attitude that we are neither the doer of
actions, nor the one who reaps their results, we'll begin to taste
the freedom that lies beyond all doing. And peace will come
flooding into our lives.

5—True Independence

Once long ago, three yogis were practicing meditation together by the side of a lake. Suddenly, the first yogi stood up and said, "Oh! I forgot my meditation cushion." He miraculously ran across the lake to retrieve it. A few minutes later, he calmly walked back across the lake with his meditation cushion safely tucked under his arm. No sooner had he returned than the second yogi stood up and said, "Oh no! I forgot to hang my clothes to dry." He too calmly walked across the water, hung his laundry, and walked back over the water to continue his meditation.

The third yogi, who was new to the ashram, thought to himself, "They must be trying to test my yogic skills." Not to be outdone, he said, "So... you both think you're so advanced because you can walk on water. Well, let it be known, I too have powers." He jumped up, ran toward the lake ... and slipped on the muddy bank, falling face-first into the water. Undeterred, he climbed out of the water, walked back several feet, got a good running start, and tumbled headlong into the water again. He tried over and over, but each time, he ended up face-first in the water. The first yogi slowly turned to the second and asked, "Do you think we should tell him where the stones are?"

The point is, if you try to stand on your own two feet without realizing the real source of power, the substratum, you'll become frustrated and fall flat on your face. We must understand that the independence we are looking for arises from the bedrock of peace and contentment *within*.

Amma is completely self-reliant because she knows she is the eternally independent Atma. As for us, we usually try to grasp happiness by fulfilling our desires. This is because we identify with the body and mind—with our emotions, our concepts, our likes, and dislikes. Our happiness then becomes dependent on fulfilling the desires of the body and the mind.

In this state, we become dependent on the world and on all the experiences that come our way. All the while the True Self, the Atma, remains totally apart, independent, and free. Its bliss remains constant and unaffected by what happens in the world. It does not depend on our health or on our spouse being nice to us. It does not depend on having a full head of hair, a skinny body, or a high-paying job. The bliss of our True Self is our inherent, independent, ever-free nature.

These days, we may think we are mature and emotionally independent, but most of us are just fooling ourselves, as the following joke shows... Once, three old ladies were sitting at the dinner table discussing the problems that come with old age.

The first lady said, "Sometimes I catch myself standing in front of the refrigerator with a jar of pickles in my hands, and I can't remember whether I should put it away or start making a sandwich."

The second lady nodded in agreement and replied, "Me too! Sometimes I find myself on the landing of the stairs and can't remember whether I was on my way up or on my way down."

"Well," said the third lady, "I sure am glad I don't have problems like that... Knock on wood." As soon as she hit her knuckles on the table for luck, she looked up and said, "That must be the door. I'll get it!"

Many of us are like the third lady in this story. We think we have it all figured out. But it's only when we honestly understand where we are that we can begin to improve and evolve.

Even when we are doing lots of seva, we must continue to fine-tune our inner attitude, so we can move forward on the path... As you know, Amma's ashram does tremendous service for the poor and needy. Through the *Amrita Kuteeram* Program, for example, the ashram has built more than 45,000 homes for the poor and needy throughout India. When the program first started, we did a lot of construction along Kerala's coastline.

Amma decided to focus on that area because many coastal residents were living in thatched huts. She was sad every time she heard mothers tell stories about leaky roofs and poor security.

However, when the brahmacharis were sent out to do the construction work, they were shocked by the ingratitude shown by some of the beneficiaries. As the brahmacharis toiled in the sun, some who were receiving new homes just stood there, watching them, not lifting a finger to help. Some even made fun of the brahmacharis and criticized their work. Full of sadness, one of the brahmacharis approached Amma and told her about the situation.

Amma's response was beautiful. She said, "Son, we are building the homes to give these people a better place to live, not for their praise or appreciation. Do your work, surrender the actions to God, and accept whatever comes." Amma's simple, profound response to this brahmachari demonstrates what true spiritual independence is.

Everything Amma does is like this. She has nothing to gain, nothing to lose. Her only aim is to help whoever needs it. Her happiness, her peace, her sense of fullness—none of it depends on what she does. Praise her, criticize her, love her, hate her—it changes nothing. She is here to fulfill her dharma, to uplift the world. No matter the world's response, she remains full, complete, blissful. By Amma's grace, may we take one step closer to true independence, remaining steady amid the shifting play of forms and appearances.

6—Equal Vision

Once, before a European Tour program, I went to Amma's room to ask about an important matter. It had snowed heavily the night before, and everything outside was covered in a blanket of snow. When I saw this through the window, I was so struck by the beauty that I asked Amma to come out and have a look. Amma responded, "What about inside? Inside is also beautiful," reminding me that true vision always perceives the beauty within.

This comment made me look around the room Amma and I were in. It was just a small locker room inside a gymnasium. The devotees had laid down some temporary carpet to cover the tiles. But Amma saw the room as beautiful, just as beautiful as all of nature covered in fresh snow.

Wherever Amma is, she always sees beauty. Sometimes it is a beauty we can all appreciate, like a snow-covered mountain or a sunset. But sometimes it is a deep, subtle beauty that we are just learning to appreciate. Amma's words that day were a teaching to me, a reminder to appreciate the ever-present divinity that is always right here, wherever we find ourselves.

The scriptures have a name for the way Amma sees things – *sama-darshanam* (equal vision). This is the way of seeing that Sri Krishna is trying to awaken within Arjuna in the Bhagavad Gita:

vidyāvinaya-sampanne brāhmaṇe gavi hastini |
śuni caiva śvapāke ca paṇḍitāḥ sama-darśinaḥ ||

The wise see a knowledgeable person, a cow, an elephant, a dog, and those who eat dogs with equal vision. (5.18)

Now we are ready to write the first verse of the Amma Gita: "The wise see with equal vision the beauty of a wooded mountain and the concrete walls of a locker room."

Amma knows there is a difference between the two. On one level, the natural beauty of the outdoors may be superior. Amma knows that. But she also sees something deeper than the beauty of name and form. She sees primordial beauty—the all-pervasive, eternal beauty that never changes. This ability to turn gently within towards our true Selves, our true beauty, helps prepare us to face life with equanimity.

7—No Guarantees

Many of the scriptures in the Indian tradition, like the Upanishads and the *Bhagavad Gita*, are presented as dialogues between the guru and his student. In these texts it is the student's thirst for knowledge that inspires the guru to impart his wisdom. Thus, the concept of preaching, of speaking without being asked, doesn't exist in *Sanatana Dharma*. Amma's satsangs follow this same principle. They are not born of Amma's desire to teach. Rather, they are a response to devotees who have humbly asked her to share her spiritual wisdom.

Actually, Amma's public talks are just one way she answers her children's questions. The truth is she finds herself answering questions almost all day long, both during darshan and in sidebars beside her chair. Many nights I get a chance to stand right next to Amma and translate for her. This seva is a real treasure, for just as the Upanishads, *Gita,* and other scriptures were born out of questions asked to the guru, Amma—the living scripture—is imparting that same eternal wisdom today. Each time I am blessed to translate for her, I am able to bear witness to that.

Let me give you a taste of this experience by sharing a lively question and answer session between Amma and two devotees. Some time back, a married couple came for Amma's darshan. They wanted to know if they were meant for each other. They didn't just want Amma to bless their marriage; they wanted Amma to "officially endorse" it. Amma laughed and said, "If you are happy, Amma is happy. But marriage is one thing that can never be guaranteed."

Amma's response here speaks not only of marriage, but of life itself, reminding us that nothing in this world can be fully relied upon. There is no guarantee or warranty on life. Life brings us all kinds of circumstances that may bring us comfort and happiness or hardship and pain. Either way, it is up to us to turn whatever comes our way to our advantage.

Amma is here to teach us that any security or happiness we receive from the world is unstable, and that the only thing that is guaranteed is the love of our True Self, God, and the guru. They are our only true source of joy and stability.

Thus, Amma is trying to help us to see the experiences of life not as an end in themselves but as a means to attain the ultimate, our True Self. When we see life this way, we are living with *viveka* (discernment rooted in proper judgment). All masters, including Amma, strive to awaken this quality in their disciples. As Vidura says in the *Mahabharata*:

na devā daṇḍam-ādāya rakṣanti paṣupālavat |
yaṁ tu rakṣitum-icchanti buddhyā saṁvibhajanti tam ||

God does not guide us with a stick like a shepherd.
Instead, he gives discernment to the one he wishes to
protect. (5.1222)

Amma urges us to use our discernment and discrimination so that we become rooted in our True Self rather than in the unstable world of appearances. This doesn't mean we have to give up our dreams. By all means, get married, have children, start businesses, and enjoy God's wonderful creation, but never see them as an end in themselves. They are merely temporary. Life and its experiences are short, often very short. And even when life is long, it is still far shorter than we think. Remember, once you make it over the hill, what happens? You pick up speed!

As a way of exploring impermanence, let's take the example of a paper coffee cup. The paper cup is important. Without it, you cannot drink your coffee. But, after you drink it, you throw away the cup. Once the coffee is gone, the cup is worthless. It's the same with our bodies. They are made so we can drink a special type of coffee, not Starbucks, or Peet's, not Tim Hortons, or Dunkin' Donuts... not even the best of all coffees, Madras Coffee. The coffee I am talking about is *jnanamritam* (the immortal nectar of the guru's wisdom). And we only have a few years left to imbibe it. If not, Mr. Death will come and crush our cup before we have even raised it to our lips.

But Amma never forces anyone to drink this coffee. Instead, she gently guides us forward by awakening our viveka, so we can begin to distinguish between the eternal and the fleeting. This is certainly how it was with all of us who came to Amma in the late 1970s. Back then, we had very little viveka. At least this was true for me!

I was like the boy in the following joke. One day a teacher asked a boy in her class, "Which is more useful, sunlight or moonlight?"

The boy answered, "What an easy question! Moonlight is more useful! It helps us to see at night. During the day, there is already light. Why do we even need the sun?"

I was the same way back then. I did not understand or value the importance of the guru, spiritual life, meditation, or studying the scriptures. But over time Amma awakened my appreciation of spirituality—not with demands, but naturally, organically, with her love, patience, and compassion.

Amma never disciplined us in the beginning. Instead, she often just started meditating. We would look at each other, shrug our shoulders, and realize maybe we should try too. This is how we were introduced to meditation.

After meditation, Amma would sing some *bhajans*, and we would join her. After a while, this became a habit for us, and we would start to feel guilty if we missed even one day. So, in a way the transformation was effortless for us. This is exactly how Amma guides her children to this day.

Of course, it is impossible to always follow Amma's perfect example and teachings. But no matter how many times we fail, she will never abandon us. She will just keep gently nudging us and encouraging us with her divine love and tender concern. Gradually, she will awaken our devotion and inspire us to deepen our commitment to spiritual life.

I would like to end this chapter with a story from the epic *Ramayana*. When Hanuman returned from Lanka with Sita's ring, proving she was alive and well, Rama was overjoyed. Do you know what Lord Rama did? He hugged Hanuman.

We may wonder why Rama only gave a hug. Rama could have showered Hanuman with material gifts. But these gifts would not have been adequate; Hanuman's service was unparalleled. It was priceless, transcending monetary value. No material thing would have been appropriate. So, all Rama could do was hug Hanuman with all his heart.

Somehow, here we all are with Amma, and even though we have not done anything much, maybe a little seva here and there, she is hugging us with complete love and compassion. We should not underestimate the transformative power of this hug. It is the most tremendous gift Amma could give us. It is the only way she can express the depth of her love for us. From another angle, Amma's hug is a symbol of our perfect union with her. Just as two become one in a hug, Amma is showing us that we are all one with her, that we too are that Self.

Amma's hug can awaken our viveka. It is a hug that can shift our focus from perishable objects to permanent, eternal bliss. This gentle embrace quietly reminds us that beyond life's uncertainties, there is an eternal reality within us that can always be trusted. So, let us all put in whatever effort we can to become a little bit more like Hanuman, a little more worthy of this most precious of treasures, Amma's hug.

8—The Light of Knowledge

In 1993, Amma was invited to address the Parliament of World Religions in Chicago. As one of Amma's Swamis, I was very proud. When the Parliament elected her president, I was even more proud. Ever since, Amma has been honored with awards, prizes and titles including the Gandhi-King Award for Non-violence, the Cinema Vérité Peace Prize, and an Honorary Doctorate of Humane Letters from SUNY (State University of New York). The list goes on and on. And each time Amma receives a prize like this, I make sure that it is quickly added to Amma's resume. (Don't worry, Amma is not looking for a new job! We swamis just like to keep a record of these things.)

There is nothing wrong with this kind of pride. We are Amma's children, and we are proud of our mother. So naturally, we are happy when we see the world recognizing her as the amazing humanitarian and spiritual leader that she is. But Amma sees all this quite differently.

In 2006 Amma received the James Parks Morton Interfaith Award in New York City. Just before she left for the ceremony, an ashram resident asked Amma how she felt about the award. Amma immediately responded that she was not at all interested in receiving anything but only in giving.

Most people these days are not like this. They are only interested in taking. This reminds me of a story. Once, a medical agent, who had been hired by a private hospital to drum up business, was on vacation in a small farming town. (If you are a medical agent, please don't be sad. This is just a joke.) Anyway, while he was walking through the streets, he saw a large crowd gathered at the scene of a road accident. The agent desperately wanted to reach the victim, so he could give him his business card. But the crowd was too thick, so he started shouting at the top of his lungs, "Let me through! Please, let me through!

I'm family. I need to be with him!" The crowd made way for the agent. When he got to the center, he saw the victim lying still in front of him. It was a dead donkey. This is what happens when we focus on taking and not on giving. We make a donkey out of ourselves.

These days many people speak and write about Amma, the humanitarian—how she gives food, clothing, shelter, and medical care to the poor and needy. But few talk about the priceless boon of *jnana danam* (the gift of knowledge) that she is bestowing on humanity. The ancient Indian sage Bhartrhari speaks of this incomparable gift in one of his poems:

> *na cora-hāryaṁ na ca rāja-hāryaṁ na bhrātṛrbhājyaṁ na ca bhārakārī |*
> *vyayē kṛte vardhata eva nityaṁ vidyādhanaṁ sarvadhanāt pradhānam ||*

It cannot be stolen by a thief, nor taxed by the government. Nor can a relative sue you for his share of it. It is not a burden to carry. And it always increases when spent. The gift of knowledge is the greatest of all gifts.

I'm sure you've all seen images of Lakshmi Devi, the goddess of wealth. If you look closely at her hands, you'll see she's forming two *mudras* (sacred gestures rich with spiritual meaning). Her left hand is in the *varada mudra*, with the palm facing outward and fingers pointing down, symbolizing compassion and giving. Her right hand is in the *abhaya mudra*, with the palm also facing outward but the fingers pointing up, offering protection and fearlessness. The varada mudra fulfills our desires and represents every material boon that money can buy—wealth, security, and pleasure. The abhaya mudra, on the other hand, bestows absolute fearlessness.

The abhaya mudra represents the perfect Self-knowledge that arises when we embrace our deathless, true nature. This is why the abhaya mudra is said to be the greater of the two, for it is through knowledge alone that we return to the source of fearlessness, our True Self. This knowledge can only come to us through a *Satguru*.

From a spiritual point of view, the material gifts of the varada mudra act like a middleman in a deal. But as any savvy businessman knows, the middleman isn't necessary. It's wiser to go straight to the source, the abhaya mudra — fearless Self-knowledge.

Once a man walked into a bar and said to the bartender, "To be honest, I don't have any money. But I do have a singing frog. If you let me have a drink on the house, I will tell it to sing for you."

The bartender looked at him dubiously and said, "Buddy, if you show me a singing frog, you can drink on the house all night long."

The man reached into the left pocket of his jacket and carefully pulled out a frog. He set the frog on the bar, snapped his fingers, and the frog began to sing. First it sang, "Let It Be" by The Beatles. Then it sang, "Rise Up" by Andra Day. And then, for its grand finale, it sang something even more amazing—a Tamil film song by A.R. Rahman called, "Chinna Chinna Aasai Siragadikkum Aasai Muthu Muthu Aasai." The bartender was amazed and happily started pouring the man free drinks.

About an hour later one of the customers in the bar approached the man and offered him $300 for the frog. The man readily agreed, and the patron joyfully left the bar with the singing frog. After seeing the whole thing, the bartender rushed over to the man and said, "Are you crazy? How could you sell that frog for only $300! I bet there are people who would have paid a million dollars for that frog."

The smiling man reached into his right pocket and carefully removed a hamster. "You see this little guy?" he said. "The frog is just a regular frog. This hamster is a ventriloquist."

So, the varada mudra, which bestows wealth and pleasure, is like the frog. While the abhaya mudra, the gift of Self-knowledge, is like the hamster. We want the hamster, the real thing, not the frog. And even if we don't want Self-knowledge just yet, we should at least understand that it is far greater than anything else we might hope to get from Amma. True knowledge calls us to look beyond fleeting comforts and surface pleasures toward the deep and lasting freedom of the Self.

9—Beyond the Game

Once a psychiatrist was giving a visitor a tour of a mental hospital. In one room, the visitor saw a bucket of water with a mug and a teaspoon next to it. "What is this?" the visitor asked.

The psychiatrist replied, "This is a test we use to gauge the sanity of incoming patients. We give each new patient this spoon and mug and then ask them to empty the bucket as quickly as possible."

The visitor said, "I see! So, if they empty the bucket with the mug, they are sane, and if they empty it with the teaspoon, they are crazy, right?"

"No," the psychiatrist replied. "The sane person dumps the water out of the bucket."

Many of us, like the visitor, might have thought that the mug was the most logical, efficient way to empty the bucket. But once we understand that dumping out the water is an option, we see that what we thought was logical was illogical. What we thought was efficient was inefficient. What we thought was sane was insane.

Ok, maybe it wasn't *completely* insane. Maybe, our thinking was "half-way sane." But you know another way to say "half-way sane"? Half-way crazy.

This bucket story is a metaphor. The bucket of our lives is filled with the water of our problems. When we see someone letting go of his difficulties with efficiency, using a mug, rather than a spoon, we are impressed. We may even look up to them thinking, 'He is so adept and skillful!' But when we meet a mahatma, we see that the solutions we used to admire were actually illogical and even half-crazy.

It is only when we meet Amma that we really understand what true sanity and logic are. This is because Amma looks at herself, the world, and every individual in a completely different way than we do.

On one level, Amma is playing the same game that we are. But, unlike us, Amma is playing a second game at the same time. It's a game aimed at remembering just one thing: that the game is just a game. Ultimately, Amma wants us to see the game for what it is, a temporary dance of appearances, a challenge to be met with wisdom and courage.

For us, the game feels like everything, and the stakes seem impossibly high. That's why we're full of tension and anxiety. But for Amma, it's all light entertainment, just a game. When we truly understand this, something shifts. The burden lifts, and we begin to transcend our imagined limitations.

In the chess game of our lives, there are five major pieces: our possessions, our profession, our family, our body, and our mind. We consider these to be ours, and their victory or defeat means everything to us.

This brings up an interesting question: what are Amma's chess pieces in this game? I would say she plays with the same five we do, but hers are not limited to Amma's own life. Her chessboard includes the possessions, professions, families, bodies, and minds of everyone in creation.

Given this, we might think that Amma's stake in the game is much higher than ours. We might imagine that her inner tension is much greater too. But in Amma, there is no tension whatsoever—no fear, no anxiety—only bliss, peace, and love. How is this possible? Because she knows life is just a game, like chess. She knows that her existence, that all of existence, is beyond the board. It is this knowledge that makes Amma so different from us.

Let me give you an example. Let's look at one of Amma's chess pieces: her body, a very important piece! From our perspective, successfully managing the body means keeping it healthy, strong, young, and beautiful.

Once a woman was admitted to the ICU, and her husband was completely distraught. The doctor gently said to him, "We are trying our best, but I cannot guarantee anything. She is completely unresponsive and seems to be in a coma."

Her husband pleaded, "Please, doctor, please save her. She is just fifty years old. Her family needs her."

No sooner had the husband spoken these words than something miraculous happened. The ECG started beeping wildly... The wife's hand moved, her lips trembled, and she resolutely said, *"I am only 49."*

Talk about emptying the bucket with a spoon! In this story the wife is striving for a very limited level of success. Even on her deathbed, she somehow thinks that being forty-nine rather than fifty is a victory.

Let me contrast this with a story from Amma's biography. When Amma first started giving darshan, her family was not happy about it. They didn't think it was right for an eighteen-year-old girl to be embracing strangers. Most of them wanted her to just stop this foolishness and get married. They felt her behavior was ruining her life and bringing a bad name to the family.

Amma's elder brother and one of her cousins were so upset that they threatened Amma's life. Approaching her with a big knife, they told her if she did not stop giving darshan, they would kill her.

Amma did not flinch. She calmly responded, "I am not afraid of death. The body must meet its end sooner or later. But it is impossible for you to kill the True Self." She went on to say that she would never stop taking care of the poor and suffering, and that they should just get on with it if they wanted to kill her. Of course, they failed. Amma's mother unexpectedly came home, and they fled in terror.

How was Amma able to remain so calm in the face of death? It was because she knows that the human body is just like a chess piece in a game. She knows that her body is not the totality of her existence; she exists far beyond the boundaries of the game.

If our lives had been threatened by two young men like this, many of us would have instinctively moved to defend ourselves. We might even have delivered a Triple Wushu Butterfly Kick to both their heads.

But responding with violence would have been like emptying the bucket with a mug. Amma is not concerned with defending her body; she tipped over that bucket long ago. She knows that she is not the body, not the mind—that she is eternal, infinite Consciousness. Her response to her brother and cousin demonstrated true skill and mastery in action.

Some of you may very well be thinking, "Swamiji, that is all very well and good, but I cannot afford to be 100% like Amma. My profession, my family, my possessions, my body, and mind are all very dear to me. And while I would eventually like to experience that my existence transcends the game board, I also need to take care of business. I cannot afford to say, 'Okay if you want to kill me, kill me. I am the True Self.' From time to time, I need to do some of those Triple Wushu Butterfly Kicks to defend myself."

To this, I would respond, "If you don't think Amma can do Triple Wushu Butterfly Kicks, you don't know Amma."

Of course, I am not talking about literal Triple Wushu Butterfly Kicks, but metaphorical ones. What I mean is that when it comes to dealing with the professional, material, mental, physical, and family problems of her children, Amma has incredible skills. She has "the skills to pay the bills" unlike anyone else on the planet.

I'll give you an example. A long time ago, there was a young man in the ashram who aspired to become a monk, but this caused a lot of tension in his family. His parents were distraught; they wanted him to get married and give them grandchildren. Eventually, it led to a big fight.

So, he came back to the ashram and poured his heart out to Amma, saying, "My parents were so mean to me, Amma! They kept insisting I get married just so they can have grandchildren. They're so selfish! Finally, I couldn't take their nagging anymore and shouted, 'Shut up!'" He looked sheepishly at Amma and continued, "Amma, my parents were shocked. I have never raised my voice to them like that before."

The young man was sure Amma would console him. And he was right, she did, but it didn't end there. Amma also instructed him to write a letter of apology to his parents.

"But Amma," he replied, "I'm *not* sorry. I wouldn't even know what to say."

"It's simple," Amma responded. "You just tell them, 'I am sorry. I should not have shouted at you. I should not have treated you so poorly.'"

"Okay," he replied. "You're right. I should not have shouted like that. I will write the letter."

But Amma was not finished: "...And you say to them, 'Mother and Father, don't you see how little control I have over my mind? Don't you see how impatient I am? How quick to anger? How disrespectful? It is because of these negativities that I have joined Amma's ashram. I want to get rid of them. I want to become patient and peaceful and learn to respect my elders. Until I learn to do that, any family life I might have would be hell for everyone. I would treat my wife and children just as disrespectfully as I treated you. So, please understand why I want to live this life. I want to refine my mind and my character. I want to become a person that both of you can be proud of.'"

This was a masterful Triple Wushu Butterfly Kick. Amma's advice was perfect. With one answer, she accomplished three things:

1) She helped the young man fulfill his dharma by apologizing to his parents.

2) She used his parents' complaints to prove to them that the young man should follow a disciplined spiritual life at the ashram.

3) She showed the young man that he still had a lot of work to do to refine his mind and gain mental equanimity.

Whatever the state of our minds, whether they are like a supercomputer or an outdated OS, Amma's mind is far more efficient. She can see every situation as it is and creates solutions that tackle many problems at once. How is this possible? It is because her mind is totally pure and refined.

Amma understands that she is the foundation of the chessboard. She is one with all the players, and she makes the rules. That is why her mind is so peaceful. That is why Amma is not limited by anxiety and fear; that is why her mind can apply itself to whatever situation arises with perfect clarity and skill.

Even though Amma knows that the game of life is not the ultimate reality, she plays the game with intensity because she is determined to uplift *us*. One blessed day with her help we will transcend the game too.

Ultimately, Amma wants us to play the game as skillfully as she does. That's why she holds nothing back. Unlike ordinary teachers who guard their secrets, Amma freely pours out everything she knows for the benefit of her children.

These days, we hear stories of professors who are afraid that their students will outpace them. Some even go so far as to claim their students' work as their own. This is never the case with a true spiritual master like Amma. Ordinary chess masters may think, "If I teach my students everything, they may defeat me one day!" Amma is completely free of such thinking. The gift of her knowledge is total, perfect, and complete.

10—Beyond the Three States

When people first meet Amma, they are deeply touched by her boundless love and compassion. What many do not realize, though, is that her grace arises from a profound source—her lived experience of the one consciousness shining in everything. Her greatness rests in this realization, in knowing herself as that consciousness.

This is the wisdom Amma tirelessly works to awaken in us, not as mere words but as living Truth. Yet to guide us toward it, words are still needed.

Of all the Upanishads, perhaps none speaks of this Truth more clearly than the *Mandukya Upanishad*. Only twelve verses long, it points directly to the Self, showing how the waking, dreaming and deep sleep states rise and fall within Om, while the underlying light of consciousness shines through as Om's very essence, ever unchanged.

The Upanishad explains that Om has four elements: 'a', 'u', 'm', and silence. In Sanskrit, 'a' and 'u' join to make 'o'. When 'm' is added, they merge into the syllable Om. All three sounds rest upon silence, which supports and pervades them. 'A' is the waking state, 'u' is the dreaming state, and 'm' is the deep sleep state. Silence is that consciousness that holds them all.

Let us look more closely at these four elements, beginning with the sound 'a'. This sound represents the waking state. Here the body acts, the senses gather impressions, and the world stretches out before us. Because this experience feels so vivid, we often take it as the whole of reality. Yet everything in waking comes and goes: roles, routines, work, family. The world, the mind, and the body all change, so they cannot be the Self. The Self is the unmoving witness behind them.

The sound 'u' represents the dream state, in which the senses rest but the mind creates a world of its own. In dreams we may fly through the sky, encounter those long gone, or wrestle with old fears. While it lasts, it feels real. Yet even in dream, we remain only the witness. When we wake and remember, "I dreamt," we realize we were always the untouched witness. Dreams pass, but the Self remains. In waking we observe the waking self. In dream we observe the dreamer. The one Self alone witnesses both waking and dream.

The sound 'm' represents deep sleep. Here there is no waking body, no dream world, only blankness. At first this might seem like emptiness, but if it were truly nothing, how could we later say, "I slept well"? Something was present, aware not of objects but of their absence. That absence cannot be the Self, for it too is observed. Even in the absence of all names and forms, the witness is present. The Self remains.

Notice the difference between waking, dreaming, and deep sleep. In waking we know a full outer world; in dream, we know an inner world; and in deep sleep we know the absence of all worlds. But all three are witnessed in the same way. The content changes, but the one who knows does not.

Every chant of Om begins and ends in silence. Without silence, Om would have nowhere to rise from and nowhere to return to. Silence exists before and after Om, and it supports the sounds as they rise and fade. In the same way, waking, dreaming, and deep sleep cannot stand on their own; they require the witness to exist.

A doubt may arise here. You may wonder, "I thought Advaita was all about unity, so why are you saying the waking, dreaming, and deep sleep states are not really me?" The Truth is that these states have no existence apart from the Self. Just as waves cannot exist without the ocean, so too waking, dreaming, and deep sleep cannot exist without consciousness. Remove the ocean, and the waves are gone. Remove consciousness, and the three states vanish with it. Even so, we often mistake these passing states for who we are. In Amma's words: "You see your reflection in a mirror, but you shouldn't mistake it for another you."

Amma often explains that Self-realization is like being fully aware during deep sleep—it is not a state of blankness, but of blissful freedom.

This is the Truth in which Amma ever abides. She sees everything in the waking world—children, trees, animals, and human beings—as her own reflections. As the *Lalita Sahasranama* proclaims, "She brings forth and dissolves countless worlds with the opening and closing of Her eyes."

The three states arise and fall like waves, while the ocean, Her underlying consciousness, remains unchanged. With boundless compassion, Amma is gently guiding us toward that same Truth. Slowly but surely, she is helping us see through her eyes of oneness, peace, and love.

As we walk along life's path, all we need to do is hold on to Amma's hand. If we can do that, the truths of the *Mandukya Upanishad* will gradually become our lived reality.

Amma's knowledge that she is the changeless Self beyond the three states is her very essence. All her glories—love, compassion, wisdom, and tireless service—arise from Her knowledge of the Self.

As we begin to assimilate this, may we too touch the same source of love, strength, and freedom that shines through her. But for this knowledge to fully blossom, we must first purify our minds of fear, attachment, and the pull of likes and dislikes.

Part 2: Spiritual Growth

11—The Root of Fear

Once, when Amma was in Chennai, a mother and father brought their son for darshan. The boy was suffering from some form of schizophrenia. His eyes were shining with frightening intensity, and he was shouting and thrashing around violently. He was so wild that it took three of his family members to restrain him as they dragged him forward for Amma's blessing. I was standing near Amma at the time, helping with translation from Tamil into Malayalam. To be honest, I began to feel a little afraid as they came close to Amma's chair. Finally, the father turned to me and said, "Swamiji, we don't know what to do about our son. He's like this all the time. The medicines are not working. Some people even think he's possessed. He can be quite violent. He has struck his mother and me several times. Sometimes he even bites us."

At this point, it was the boy's turn for darshan, and my heart was beating fast. But Amma was as cool as a cucumber. Even after I told Amma that the boy sometimes bites people, she remained relaxed. Here I was, two feet away, full of tension, and there was Amma relaxed and blissful with this mentally ill boy's mouth resting right against her neck.

Of course, tense situations are quite common around Amma. From time to time when things like this happen, I ask Amma if she is afraid. But every single time I've asked, Amma just laughs at me as if to say, "What? Fear is not in my vocabulary."

The scriptures proclaim *dvitīyād vai bhayaṁ bhavati* (Fear is born out of the feeling of duality.) One who has Self-knowledge sees only himself wherever he looks. And so, wherever Amma looks, she sees only her Self. When one perceives the world this way, where is there a separate person to be afraid of? It's not that Amma doesn't see the birds, the trees, and the people. Of course, Amma sees all this, but she never loses sight of the underlying oneness of creation. This is what Amma's smile communicates. When we closely watch her, we see that there is no gap between Amma's knowledge of unity and the way she acts. With us it is rarely like this. With us, there is usually a very big gap.

Long ago, a lady came to share her problems with Amma. Back then Amma was giving darshan in a thatched hut right next to her house. Anyway, this lady and her neighbors were not getting along at all. It had reached the point that the neighbors were physically threatening this lady. Amma told her not to be afraid. The woman replied, "No, no, no, Amma, I'm not afraid. Anyway, with you in my life, what is there to be afraid of?" The lady was so immersed in her conversation with Amma that she did not notice the long black snake that had begun sliding through the thatched leaves right above her. A few devotees *did* notice and shouted, "Snake! Snake!" Instantly the woman, who had just professed fearlessness, broke free of Amma's embrace and ran to the back of the hut. Amma stayed seated right where she was and gently laughed as the snake slithered away.

There is nothing wrong with fear in itself. It is a natural reaction to dangerous circumstances. It is a God-given alarm system that prompts us to act. But once this instinct has played its role, fear should leave us, and our calm, rational mind should return. Fear should go after it has served its purpose.

Amma says that each one of us has our own set of emotional problems. For some of us it may be fear, for others anger, or jealousy, or guilt, or greed, or impatience... The list goes on. But how do we move from knowing we have these negativities to actually releasing them? How do we convert this knowledge into emotional strength? One way is to introspect and to realize that these negative qualities are not who we really are. We are the eternal Atma that continues even after death.

If we can remain aware that we are the Atma—infinite Being, Consciousness, and Bliss—greed, jealousy, and fear will begin to melt away all on their own. If we can remain aware that the Atma is the same in everyone, anger and aversion will dissolve. All that this method requires is a little introspection to find our problem spots, followed by a mental affirmation of who we really are. But in order to truly remember the Self, we must work hard to purify our minds and let go of negativities.

12—The Sweeper

I remember being in Durgapur with Amma during her 2004 North Indian Tour. Darshan had finished about eight hours before, and everyone was waiting for Amma to come down and get into her camper so that the caravan could continue on to Kolkata. But Amma loves to go off script. No sooner had she come down the stairs than she turned to us and asked, "What have you been doing all morning? Why didn't you clean up the school grounds?"

We looked around and saw a big mess—a field full of paper plates, plastic cups, and other trash. Amma immediately began cleaning it up herself, and we all joined in. Soon more than two hundred people were in full action, picking up all the trash and waste. At one point, Amma saw a pile of rotten potato curry. She reached into it with her bare hands and began putting it into a trash bag. Seeing her do this, one of the *brahmacharinis* tried to stop her saying, "Amma, please stop. That will make your hands itch." It was hard to watch Amma touching something so dirty, but Amma would not stop. While scooping up yet more curry from the ground, Amma turned and said, "My body is made of the same five elements as yours." Then she added, almost inaudibly, "The only difference is my mind."

We are more similar to Amma than we may think. Amma's body is composed of flesh and bone just like ours. On the level of the Atma, we are like her too. We are the True Self every bit as much as she is. This may sound irreverent, but is it not the main teaching of spirituality that there is only one True Self shared by all? And yet, while this is the truth, we still feel a big difference between Amma and ourselves. Wrapping our minds around this is like a big riddle.

Luckily, Amma herself gave the answer: the *only* difference between her and us is the mind. That being said, Amma's mind is radically different from ours. She is able to remain totally peaceful, happy, caring, loving, helpful, and selfless because her mind is perfectly refined. As the saying goes, "As the mind, so the man."

It is said that the typical human mind has three natural defects:

- *Mala:* impurities such as selfish desires, anger, greed, and jealousy
- *Vikshepa:* agitation and restlessness
- *Avarana:* ignorance

The spiritual path aims to remove these three defects, and Amma has come to help us do just that.

This brings to mind one of Amma's many visits to the United Nations in New York. While there, a journalist asked her what she would do if she became the leader of the world. Amma replied, "I would be a sweeper." In India, a sweeper is someone who goes with a broom through the halls of offices, universities, government buildings, and even roadsides to sweep. Naturally, the journalist looked a bit confused when Amma gave this response. To be honest, we were all a bit confused.

Amma noticed and clarified, "I would sweep the minds of the world clean."

Actually, this is what Amma is already doing. She has dedicated her life to sweeping away our mala, vikshepa, and avarana: our mental impurities, our agitation, and our ignorance. Amma is laser-focused on this because she knows that the mind is crucial in spiritual life. It is the stage on which we perform our life's drama. If the stage, our mind, is shaky, our performance will be weak.

So, how do we begin to clear away the first layer of negativity, mala, which includes anger, greed, desire, and selfishness? Amma recommends daily journaling.

Here's just one story of an ashramite who took Amma's advice to heart. Like many other devotees, he began journaling every day, as Amma still suggests, and it changed his life.

This ashramite had a serious anger problem and often expressed his rage through harsh, cutting words. Sometimes he really gave it to people. One day, after yet another outburst, Amma told him to start keeping a diary. Each night before bed, he was to reflect on his day and note down the moments he had lost his temper alongside the moments he had brought joy to others. Amma encouraged him to treat this process like a businessman looking over the books to keep track of his profits and losses. Amma said this would help him bring more awareness into his day-to-day life. The process completely transformed him. These days, you would never know that he had once had a serious anger problem.

We can all benefit from keeping a diary like this. Just choose a spiritual quality you want to cultivate, or a negativity you want to eliminate, and write about it every night. When you wake up the next morning, bring that quality to mind. If it's a quality you want to nurture, reflect on specific ways it supports your spiritual path. If it's a negativity you want to eliminate, consider how it harms you and those around you. Finally, take a vow to make progress on your chosen quality throughout the day.

When you write in this nightly diary, try writing directly to Amma, as if you were speaking to her. This way, you will not only reduce your negativities but also deepen your bond with Amma.

As I mentioned earlier, mahatmas like Amma attract us just as magnets attract iron. If you rub an iron filing against a magnet long enough, it too becomes magnetized. Similarly, if we rub our rusty personalities against Amma's divine personality long enough, her divine qualities will eventually awaken in us. I will give you one example from my own life.

When I first came to the ashram, I knew nothing about spirituality or the proper way of showing respect to a mahatma like Amma. I also did not appreciate just how wise Amma was in all fields of knowledge. I understood she was a spiritual master, but I thought Amma lacked experience and knowledge about practical matters. Whereas I, who had worked for a few years in a bank, knew all about the world. And so, I often argued with Amma about the practical aspects of running the ashram. I was very foolish back then, but I was in my twenties, when many youngsters think they know everything but actually know very little. I was foolish beyond foolish.

But in my defense, Amma never said things like, "Hey, you should respect me," or "You should prostrate before me," or "You should behave properly in my presence." In the beginning, Amma never imposed discipline on us. That was to come later.

Anyway, one day Amma said something that I didn't agree with, and I started arguing back. In those days when someone argued with Amma or disobeyed her, she usually didn't object. But on that day, Amma stood her ground, saying, "No, what you are saying is *not* correct!" This threw me off guard, but I was in no mood to admit defeat. By the end of the conversation, I was all revved up. Suddenly, Amma got up and went to her room. Even then, I didn't want to stop arguing; I wanted to *win*. So, I jumped to my feet and followed Amma. She had closed the door to her room, but not completely. When I looked in, I could see that Amma was in meditation. It was impossible to continue the argument.

Thinking Amma would come out of her room soon, I waited outside, so I could continue where I had left off. I waited for fifteen minutes, but Amma kept meditating. Forty-five minutes passed; Amma was still meditating. I didn't have the patience to wait any longer, and so I decided to continue the argument later.

Amma came out of her room after two and a half hours of meditation. By that time, I was in a nearby town buying supplies for the ashram. Even after all that time to reflect, I still thought I was right and wanted to prove it to her. But despite my anger and arrogance, I was quite impressed that Amma could meditate after such an argument, as though nothing had happened.

Two long weeks passed before I had a chance to speak with Amma again. By then, I realized I had behaved improperly. I apologized saying, "Amma, after that heated argument, you went to your room and became immersed in meditation. I, on the other hand, struggled for ten days, unable to meditate properly. As soon as I closed my eyes, the only thing I could think of was how to defeat you in that argument. I meditated on this for ten days! How was it possible for you to effortlessly meditate immediately after that fight?"

Amma replied, "As soon as I realized it was a waste of time to argue with a useless fellow like you, my mind became introverted. A split second is enough for me to go within."

Her words cut through my ego and revealed how different her mind is from mine. A beautiful commentary on the *Bhagavad Gita* illuminates this difference:

"The guru is not like the disciple. The disciple must make a firm resolve to renounce his negativities. But for the guru, there is no such renunciation. It is the other way around: Seeing the master's Self-knowledge, the negativities themselves become disheartened. They know there is no place for them in the guru's heart, and it is the negativities who renounce the guru."

So, negativities have renounced Amma, but we are in a different boat. We must consciously *choose* to renounce our negativities.

If we want our mind to be strong and steady, we must also sweep away the second mental defect, vikshepa (agitation). In spirituality, having a peaceful, focused mind is essential. We can nurture such a mind by meditating, chanting our mantra, doing *archana*, and singing bhajans. But why are these practices so helpful? Because each of them requires concentration. Performing them is like weightlifting for the mind. If practiced regularly, they slowly increase the mind's ability to concentrate. Amma often highlights this saying, "The remote control of our mind must rest firmly in the palm of our hand."

I once heard a good joke along these lines. Why are people like teabags? Because they only know how strong they are when they get into hot water. The corona pandemic, with its lockdowns and restrictions, put us all in hot water and showed us exactly where we stand in spiritual life. It taught us about our society and, more importantly, about ourselves.

During the pandemic, millions and millions of people became physically, emotionally, and intellectually agitated. When our environment becomes disturbed, we suddenly realize we can't find permanent peace or happiness outside ourselves. It is only then that we realize the importance of making our minds peaceful. Our bodies may be forced into lockdown, but our minds should always be free. If we allow our negative mental habits and tendencies to overwhelm us, then we ourselves have chosen to put our minds in lockdown. But if we can learn to imbue our thoughts and actions with positive creativity, our minds will remain free, capable of transcending any challenge that arises.

Amma's mind cannot be confined because it is completely under her control. That inner mastery is what allowed her to remain steady and compassionate during the pandemic, even as the world around her struggled with fear and isolation. She stayed focused on uplifting the minds and hearts of all her children.

In Amritapuri, Amma created an atmosphere of joy despite the strict lockdown. One brahmachari put it this way: "In Amritapuri, Amma turned corona season into mango season."

His words captured the feeling perfectly, for in India, everyone celebrates when mangoes begin to ripen on the trees. After all, everyone knows that mangoes, especially Indian mangoes, are among the tastiest fruits in the world. Somehow, even in those tense and uncertain days, Amma brought that same sweetness to the ashram.

But the sweetness of Amma's love and joy didn't stop at the ashram gates. Amma shared the exact same joy and love with her children around the world, many of whom were struggling with fear, depression, and isolation. To uplift them, she started streaming her satsangs, bhajans, and meditations online. She offered online retreats and classes on everything from permaculture to *tabla*; Malayalam to Sanskrit; mantra chanting to cooking. Amma did all of this with only one aim: to help her children focus their minds and transcend the lockdown.

Despite all of Amma's efforts, some of us came to realize that we still lack control over our minds. That's okay! It's important to see where we are, so we can grow. By God's grace, the pandemic passed. Amma says the world should see it as both a wake-up call and a lesson. It reminded us to care for the outer world by nurturing the environment, and it pointed to the inner work we must do to master our own minds. Only then will we know peace.

Once, a scientist riding in a boat turned to the boatman and asked in a smug tone, "Have you ever studied physics?"

"No," the boatman replied.

"Then half your life has gone to waste," the scientist said flatly.

Soon a storm tossed up great waves, and the boat began to fill with water. "Do you know how to swim?" the boatman shouted.

"No!" cried the scientist.

"Then your entire life is about to go to waste."

It's a light story, but it makes a serious point. We must remove agitation from our mind. Only then will we be able to see life as a play, no matter how stormy it gets. Amma puts it this way: "An experienced swimmer takes great pleasure swimming in the ocean, but someone who doesn't know how to swim will drown in the waves."

The third and final impurity Amma is trying to sweep away from our minds is avarana (ignorance). In fact, it is the last obstacle between us and total spiritual liberation. When confronting ignorance, having a guru like Amma is essential. She is the embodiment of supreme knowledge, and only someone like her, who has assimilated this knowledge, can bestow it on us.

Amma's knowledge is what makes her who and what she is. All of the beautiful, wondrous, and mystifying things about Amma—her darshan, her compassionate service, her tireless love for all—all of these are born out of her supreme wisdom. They manifest because Amma knows her true inner nature through and through. She knows she is the absolute reality: pure Existence, pure Consciousness, pure Bliss. Amma is here to help us understand that this is our nature too. As the saying goes, "The seeker is that which he seeks."

Several years ago, during darshan on an Indian tour, a seven-year-old girl approached Amma from the side. It was quite crowded, but somehow this girl made her way up to Amma's chair. Eventually, the little girl leaned in towards Amma to ask a question. Amma smiled and leaned way over, so the girl could speak directly into her ear. Everyone watched as Amma listened intently to the little girl.

As soon as the little one finished speaking, Amma turned to those nearby and said, "Her father says Amma is Kali, but her mom says that Amma is their mother. She wants to know who is right!"

Amma, delighted by the girl's innocence, laughed good-naturedly, then lovingly pinched the girl's cheek, and said, "Do you want to know who Amma is?"

The girl's eyes widened. "Yes," she whispered breathlessly.

Amma replied, "If you want to know who Amma is, then know who *you* are."

Amma gave the girl quite an assignment. Knowing who we are is no small task! It requires us to clean away the impurity of ignorance by meditating and diving deep into Amma's teachings and scriptures like the *Bhagavad Gita*. Only then will we finally know through and through that Amma is our very own Self. Only then will we become one with Amma and enjoy eternal darshan.

Amma's wisdom makes her glorious! One day, that same wisdom will fill our lives with fullness and joy too. Any satisfaction or contentment we seem to find in the world around us never lasts for long. If we want to feel truly whole, we must turn to the source within.

Actually, when we think we are enjoying worldly objects, we are really experiencing our True Self through them. Attaining the things we desire simply quiets the turbulence of our mind for a while, allowing the bliss of our True Self to shine through *temporarily*. We may find it hard to believe that the objects we hold so dear contain no happiness in themselves, and that all bliss comes from within. But whether you believe it or not, it is true. Let me share an example to shed some light on this.

Imagine it's 10:00 p.m. and you go to bed for the night. You have to wake up at 4:30 a.m. to get to archana on time. So, you set your alarm. Soon you are deep asleep. The next thing you know, for some reason, you wake up. The room is pitch black. You cannot see anything, and you are not sure what time it is. It could be that you've only been asleep an hour or so, or it could be 4:29 a.m.! Saying a quick prayer, you reach towards the nightstand beside your bed and feel around for your phone. You find it, take it in your hand, and bring it before your eyes. You swipe.

It's 11:30 p.m.! You still have five-and-a-half hours to sleep!

Moments like these are perhaps the happiest of our lives. Why is that? There is no delicious food in deep sleep. There are no beach resorts, no beautiful people, no money, no name, no fame. There aren't even dreams. There's just nothingness. Yet, somehow, when we wake up, we know that nothing is more blissful than deep sleep.

The saints and sages say our memory of blissful deep sleep is proof that all happiness comes from within us alone. What keeps us from abiding in that same bliss throughout our waking life are our desires, which constantly agitate our mind.

Someone once asked Amma what Self-realization was like. Amma replied, "It's like experiencing the bliss of deep sleep while you are wide awake."

In Self-realization we abide in eternal bliss, no matter what is happening in the outside world. It is, in Amma's words, "a feeling of complete fullness, with absolutely nothing else to gain. It is a realization that makes life perfect." This is what we, as spiritual seekers, are after. And it is the knowledge of who we are and who we are not that will lead us there. It is the only way. Amma has always understood this truth through and through, and it has made her totally free and blissful. She is trying to guide us to the same Truth.

Perhaps now we can better understand why the mind is everything. It is the source of bondage, and it is the source of freedom. To move toward that freedom, we must commit to purifying ourselves by sweeping away negativity, agitation, and ignorance from the mind. Only then can we truly begin to rise.

13—Refining Our Worship

A few years ago, a young man came for Amma's darshan. Amma held him very sweetly, like she does everyone, stroked his chest a few times, and asked him to sit on the stage for a while. The young man, who was about ten feet from Amma, sat quietly for fifteen minutes. Then, out of nowhere, he began shouting horrible things at Amma.

Actually, he was cursing, using all sorts of swear words and profanities. The devotees sitting near him were horrified and jumped up to remove him from the stage, but Amma turned around and said, "Let him stay." Seeing Amma's deep compassion and love, the young man calmed down. When he finally got up to leave, I went over and asked him, "Hey, why did you start shouting and swearing like that?"

He replied, "I'm sorry, Swamiji, but I am very angry about where the world is headed. Politics seems to be devolving into constant bipartisan attacks. The environment has gone past the tipping point, and I don't see things getting any better. The relationships between nations and religions seems to be getting worse and worse. I am worried about where everything is heading. I hear Amma is supposed to be the Mother of the Universe! If that's true, why isn't she doing anything about it? If I cannot express my heart to Amma, then who is there for me to share with?"

I understood his point but was not at all okay with how he expressed himself.

About an hour later, as I was standing by Amma's side, I said, "Amma, I don't understand how you can be so patient with people. I know you can accept everything, but that young man shouted so disrespectfully at you earlier! Amma, isn't there a limit?"

Amma looked up at me and said, "Who are you to judge him? You used to speak to me like that too!"

This really took me by surprise. Although I have never sworn or used foul language when speaking with Amma, it is true that in my twenties, when I first came to the ashram, I was very adamant and stubborn. Back then, I argued with Amma more than anyone else, usually about her decisions regarding ashram matters. I also frequently complained that she wasn't paying enough attention to me.

Despite this, Amma always treated me with love. She never reacted. She never scolded me. She never told me to get lost. The only thing I remember is that when I shouted, and fought, and complained, Amma would always pick up a handful of pebbles from the ground and gently cast them, one by one, on the sand in front of her. Years later, I asked Amma, why she did this—why she cast the stones.

She responded, "Son, I have only one desire for my children ... that they should purify their mind of all its negativities and rejoice in the bliss of the Self. Only then can they become offerings to the world. You had a deep-rooted anger issue back then. I wanted you to outgrow that. So, each angry word that you said to me, I offered as a mantra to God. I visualized that each stone I cast was a flower offered on your behalf."

Such is the compassion and patience of Amma. She takes all of our negativity and converts it into virtue. It doesn't matter how much dross we hold inside of us, Amma will not stop until all of it has been converted into gold. Amma doesn't care how long this takes. She will stay with us until the end of the process, even if she has to take a thousand births to do so.

In the *Bhagavad Gita*, Lord Krishna touches upon the same truth. He assures us that God accepts all our worship, even the basest and most immature, and uplifts us until our worship rises to the greatest height. All the truths the scriptures proclaim about the nature of God, we find reflected in Amma and her relationship with us. Just like Krishna, Amma accepts our desire-filled worship and gradually transforms it into worship that is pure and selfless.

This is why Amma suggests that we direct all our emotions and feelings, even the negative ones, towards God, or the guru. This will help rid us of all our negative tendencies. Amma says, "If you feel angry, direct your anger towards God. If you feel sad, direct your sorrow towards God. Sit in front of your altar and express everything in your heart to God, like a small child opening up before his mother. This will greatly unburden your heart and restore a sense of peace and calm."

With this background, let's finish the story of the young man who shouted at Amma. A few days after his outburst, the same young man came for darshan again. This time he was very calm and respectful. After his darshan, he sat by Amma's side, calm and relaxed. Five minutes later, he approached Amma with great love and respect and apologized for his harsh words.

Later that evening, Amma said to me, "You see? If I had rejected him and his way of speaking to me, where would he have gone? Does a mother ever reject her child if he shouts at her?" (Amma went on to say that if she hadn't let him take his anger out on her, he would have unleashed it on someone else. He might even have ended up in jail.)

Amma takes on our basest negativities, our most selfish desires, our darkest emotions and uplifts them. This is the essence of the true guru. Amma says that rejecting people like that young man would be like building a state-of-the-art hospital and then putting up a sign out front that says, "NO SICK PEOPLE ALLOWED!"

In fact, in Kodungallur, Kerala, there is a Kali festival centered around this very concept. During that week, people come to the Bhagavati Devi Temple to shout and curse at the Divine Mother

Kali. The things many of them say are unrepeatable; some even come to the temple drunk. Most of those who participate are not regular temple-goers. They come only during that week because shouting and expressing their anger towards God brings them a sense of solace. It was the expansive vision of mahatmas that inspired this tradition. This festival provides one week a year for everyone and anyone to communicate with God in a way that comes naturally to them. It is a good thing because it gives them a reason to come to the temple and talk to God. By meeting them where they are and accepting them as they are, God can gradually uplift them toward maturity, purity, and selflessness.

Amma, our Kali, operates exactly the same way. No matter how low our level, she comes to us and lifts us up. But please don't misunderstand. This doesn't mean Amma will do all the work for us. Even though she will come down to our level, we must still do our part and put in sincere effort if we really want to rise.

In the *Bhagavad Gita*, Lord Krishna compares the flowering of devotion to a four-step ladder. On the bottom rung of the ladder, devotees ask for things like the removal of illnesses and solutions to their problems. We can think of this as "hot water devotion" because it often arises when we are in deep trouble and want to escape suffering.

On the next rung of devotion, which is a bit higher, devotees ask for boons from God, like promotions at work, entrance to a good college, or help getting married. This kind of devotion is a step above 'hot water devotion' because we are remembering God while living in the world. We are choosing to let God in on our desires!

This reminds me of a true story. A few years ago, a devotee was talking with Amma. She seemed very moved by his innocence and goodness. With a big smile on her face Amma said, "Son, what would you like from Amma. I will give you anything."

After forty-five years with Amma, there is one thing I know for sure. Amma can do anything; she can give us anything. From my perspective, this was a golden chance for this devotee to ask for spiritual progress. I waited curiously to hear what he would ask for. Would it be spiritual understanding? World peace? Liberation?

Do you know what he asked for? Canadian citizenship! It's okay. I am not judging him. Canadian citizenship has practical value. And this devotee simply did not feel complete without it. Night after night he lay awake, tossing and turning, dissatisfied with his nationality. Of course, within a year, he got his Canadian citizenship. But it wasn't long before "Canadian citizenship desire" was replaced by another desire. Now, there was something else keeping him up at night.

Now that he was Canadian, he wanted a nice wife. So, he came back to Amma to ask for that too. With Amma's grace, he is now happily married. So far, he has not asked Amma for anything else, but I strongly suspect he will. One fulfilled desire always leads to another desire.

This reminds me of a joke. One day, a man found a brass lamp. And of course, he rubbed it three times and out popped a genie.

"Thank you," said the genie. "You have freed me from the lamp. I will grant you one boon."

"Hmmm...," said the man. "Well, I live in Southern California, but I also have a place in Hawaii. It's very expensive to fly back and forth. Please build me a bridge from Southern California to Hawaii, so I can drive there."

The genie was shocked. "Look," he said, "That is impossible. Do you know how many tons of steel and cement it would take to build that bridge?! The distance is more than 2,600 miles! Ask me for something else."

The man thought and said, "Well, okay... How about this? My relationship with my wife is sometimes a bit strained. I think this is because I never seem to know what she is really thinking. Please give me a boon to understand her emotions."

The genie stared blankly into space for several seconds and finally said, "How many lanes do you want on that bridge to Hawaii?"

My point is that even if this devotee is content with his marriage now, like the man in the joke, other marriage-related desires are waiting just around the corner. Real contentment is never possible through the fulfillment of such desires. This is something the saints and sages proclaim with absolute certainty.

Amma has her own special way of helping us to climb from desire-based devotion to spiritual devotion. She does this by giving us the material objects we ask for and then lets us experience for ourselves that they fall short. Please don't misunderstand, I'm not saying that Amma gives us defective things on purpose. We are the ones who continue to ask for them because we don't yet understand that they can never bring real, lasting happiness.

Once a man walked into a corner store and asked for twenty single cigarettes. The clerk said, "Sir, why don't you just buy a pack? You would save a lot of money. We charge 50% extra on the loosies."

The man replied, "What kind of a fool do you think I am? Money isn't everything! The ones that come in packs cause lung cancer, heart disease, liver cancer, and strokes. I'm happy to spend the extra 50% to get ones that don't cause all that!"

Of course, loose cigarettes cause those very same problems. They just come without the warning label that reminds people of the risks. The guru is like that warning label. She helps us get what we want but also reminds us that the material things we crave are limited and flawed by their very nature.

What the guru really wants to give us is dispassion. So, when we ask her for things, she may give them to us, but she always adds a hidden lesson to loosen our attachment to them. It's kind of like she mixes a laxative into everything she gives us. We want chocolate, but the guru wants to purge our desire for it. So, when we ask for chocolate, she gives us high quality chocolate mixed with a laxative. We get to eat the chocolate, but as we do, the very desire for it begins to fade. And, slowly but surely, we begin to understand that material objects can never bring real happiness.

If we want money, the guru will help us get money. But she will also help us see that money brings with it a host of problems. As the expression goes, "More money...more problems." If we want a promotion, the guru will help us get a promotion, but she will also help us see that promotions never bring real contentment. The peon wants to be a clerk, the clerk an officer, the officer a boss, the boss the owner. And on and on it goes...

This is why the only intelligent prayer is for Self-realization. For when that dawns, all our nagging desires will come to an end, and true peace and happiness will shine forth. Anything else Amma gives us will leave us wanting.

The state of dispassion towards which Amma is leading us is beautifully and simply expressed in the Narada *Bhakti Sutras*:

yat-prapya na kimcidvacchati na socati na dveshti, na ramate notsahi bhavati ||

Upon attaining this, one wants nothing else, suffers nothing, hates nothing, takes delight in nothing else, and is never excited about anything else.

Does that sound boring—not being excited about anything, not wanting anything? Actually, it's not boring at all. In the state of dispassion, there is constant delight in the one thing you do have: your own blissful Self. And the way to that bliss is through Self-knowledge alone. The *Mundaka Upanishad* does concede that this peace and contentment might be attained by other means, but only under one condition: that you manage to roll up the sky like a carpet and tuck it under your armpit. Thus, Self-knowledge is the only path to liberation.

The next rung of devotion marks the threshold into spiritual life. On this rung of the ladder, when spiritual seekers sing God's praises, do selfless service, meditate on God, chant mantras, or study the scriptures, they still hope to benefit, but in a spiritual rather than a material way. The goal at this level is to know God, to become one with God.

The final and highest rung of the devotional ladder is the rarefied state where Amma abides. At this level, there is nothing to ask of God, for only God remains. The devotee and God have merged. Such a person lives only to help others. This highest level of devotion is what we must ultimately strive for —there is nothing higher.

Now, even though Krishna describes four kinds of devotion, each higher than the last, he says very clearly that devotees from all four levels are *sukritinah janah* (noble-hearted souls). In the same way, no matter what our level, Amma is happy with us and sees us as good and admirable children. But like any loving mother, she also wants to see each of us reach our potential, and that requires sustained effort on our part.

Usually, in the beginning stages, our devotion is selfish. This is fine. It's far better than having no devotion at all. Still, Amma encourages us to keep growing. Over time, she will guide us from selfish devotion, aimed at material gain, to selfless devotion. And in the end, she will lead us beyond devotion itself, into the purity of selflessness.

14—The Spectrum of Attraction

In our lives, we naturally feel attracted to various people, places, and things. Most of these attractions are short-lived. We may like some people because of their physical appearance, but when that physical beauty begins to fade away, the attraction vanishes. Such is the fleeting nature of life.

Many years ago, before I joined the ashram, a famous actress made a public appearance near where I lived in Tamil Nadu. She was at the peak of her career, and a long line of young people were waiting for a handshake, autograph, and photo with her. Recently, when I returned to that city, the same actress was attending a program there. Now that she is a senior citizen, the only people who showed interest in her were a couple of paid secretaries. All the youngsters there were crowded around a much younger actress. The young actress was aglow with all the attention and adoration, blissfully unaware that one day she would suffer the same fate as the lonely old actress.

Recently, I read that one of today's most popular young actresses said she would undergo plastic surgery the very moment the first wrinkle appears on her face. But what is the point of this? It is simply putting off the inevitable.

Once a middle-aged woman had a heart attack and was taken to the hospital. While on the operating table she had a near-death experience. Seeing God, she asked, "Is my time up?"

God replied, "Actually, no. You have another forty-three years, two months and eight days to live."

The woman was so overjoyed at the news that she decided to stay in the hospital and have a face-lift, liposuction, and a tummy tuck. She even had someone come in to change her hair color and brighten her teeth! Since she had so much more time to live, she figured she might as well make the most of it. After her last cosmetic operation, she was released from the hospital.

On her way home, while crossing a street, she was struck and killed by an ambulance.

When she appeared in front of God this time, she said, "I thought you said I had another forty-three years to live? Why didn't you pull me out of the path of that ambulance?"

God replied, "I didn't recognize you."

Although physical attraction can be captivating at first, it inevitably fades. But this isn't the only kind of attraction we encounter. We can also be attracted to people's personalities, talents, or intellectual gifts. While this type of attraction lasts longer than physical attraction, it too eventually fades. When two people divorce due to 'irreconcilable differences,' we know that these subtler kinds of attraction have evaporated as well.

Lucky for us, there is a third type of attraction—attraction to the *Atman*. This is the attraction we feel when we look at Amma. No matter what Amma is saying or doing, people cannot take their eyes off her. Most of us, though, have to work hard to keep others' attention. Comedians, for example, have to be continuously funny, or people will stop listening to them.

But with Amma, it is not like this. Even when she is doing ordinary things, everyone around her is riveted. People even line up just to watch Amma walk to the evening program. Although many of these people have seen Amma enter the hall many times, perhaps hundreds of times, they never tire of seeing her walk.

Let me share one example from Amma's 2007 Indian Tour. After a long darshan, Amma decided to make a traditional Kerala sweet called *unniyappam* for everyone. Word spread quickly, and soon the rooftop where Amma was frying the sweets was filled with devotees. For the next half hour or so, five hundred adults watched Amma cook unniyappam. Not much was said, but everyone was enthralled. The group hung on Amma's every movement, every gesture. Objectively speaking, it was just a woman cooking snacks, so why was everyone so captivated?

Amma explains it this way: "When we see a ripe fruit, it always looks juicy and appealing. And, when we see a fully blossomed flower, it always looks beautiful and attractive. The one who has known the true nature of the Self is like a fully ripened fruit or a fully bloomed flower."

Each of the divine qualities of an enlightened one is like a petal on such a flower. And so, if we ask ten people why they are attracted to Amma, we may hear ten different answers. Some are attracted to Amma's patience, others to her humility, or her innocence, her purity, her compassion, her unconditional love, her ability to clearly explain spiritual truths.

Saints and scriptures also celebrate the mysterious attractive power of the enlightened sage. A famous saint from Tamil Nadu expressed it this way: "One who conquers one's self—to him all others will be drawn." The scriptures say the same thing.

The *Shivananda Lahari* says that the *jivatman* (individual soul) is attracted to the *Paramatman* just as iron filings are attracted to a magnet:

aṅkōlaṁ-nija-bījasantatirayaskāntōpalaṁ-sūcikā
sādhvīnaijavibhuṁlatākṣitiruhaṁ-sindhuḥ sarid-vallabham |
prāpnōtīhayathātathāpaśupatēḥ-pādāravinda-dvayaṁ
cētōvṛttirupētya-tiṣṭhati-sadāsābhaktirityucyate ||

Like the real seed progeny reaches for the mother
ankola tree,
Like the iron needle reaches for the lodestone.
Like the chaste woman reaches for her lord,
Like the tender creeper reaches for nearby trees,
Like the river reaches for the sea,
If the spirit of the mind
Reaches for the lotus feet of Pasupathi,

And stays there always,
Then that state is called devotion. (verse 61)

In Amma's Malayalam bhajan, "*Manase Nin Svantamayi,*" she shares the same truth, singing, "The Lord will attract devotion-soaked souls like a magnet attracts iron." In the same bhajan, Amma goes on to say that it is always the soul that we are attracted to. She sings, "Even the sweetheart for whom you have been struggling, without even caring for your life, even she will be frightened by your dead body and will not accompany you on your journey after death."

When the soul is no longer in the body, our attraction to it disappears. This reveals that we love the body only because of the soul that animates it—our natural attraction is always for the soul, never for the body.

This same truth helps explain the magnetic power of a mahatma. A mahatma helps us feel our attraction to the soul much more strongly than an ordinary person ever could. This is why the mahatma's physical features and accomplishments are ultimately not that important. Of course, Amma is beautiful, talented, and hardworking, but there have been many mahatmas who were not. In fact, one famous twentieth century Master, Ramana Maharshi, remained still and silent, without engaging in much outward activity at all. He often simply sat around in a loincloth reading the newspaper. But people continued pouring in to see him. His magnetic presence, soaked with peace and love, drew people from far and wide.

In our day-to-day life, though, appearances often deceive us. In fact, it was once said that "looks are so deceptive that people should have their ingredients clearly labeled, like food items in the grocery store." Imagine if everyone's inner ingredients were clearly labeled. How helpful this would be! For example, if a very handsome man had a label, you could see that he contained only 10% of the recommended daily allowance of kindness and

200% of the daily allowance of jealousy. If these qualities could be seen, how many women would fawn over him?

Or suppose you meet a physically beautiful woman. Be careful, you may well discover that she contains only 5% of the recommended daily allowance of patience, and 250% of the allowance of anger. Unfortunately, human beings do not come with such labels. That's why we must learn to carefully discern the inner qualities of others.

Of course, the most positive possible attraction we can experience is to a mahatma, whose ingredient list would read like a multivitamin of positive qualities with 1000% of the recommended daily allowance of patience, love, kindness, compassion, and peace... and 0% of the negative qualities that most of us wrestle with. Amma says, "Even a single glance, word, or action from a mahatma can benefit us." When we are attracted to a mahatma, our whole life changes for the better.

But the story doesn't end there, for there is a fourth type of attraction—the attraction of God or the Guru towards their devotees. On Amma's last European Tour, shortly before *Devi Bhava* darshan was about to begin, Amma suddenly said, "My mind keeps being drawn toward Amritapuri, towards my children back in the ashram." I did not give too much importance to the comment, but later, after the Devi Bhava darshan had finished, Amma spoke to the ashram residents through a webcam.

Back in Amritapuri, a big screen was set up for the residents to see Amma. Simultaneously, Amma could see all the faces of her ashram children on her laptop screen. Seeing them gathered there, Amma said, "It has been weeks since I have seen you. Do you have anything to share with Amma?" Hearing this, with one voice, the brahmacharis and brahmacharinis cried out, "Ammaaaa! Ammaaaa!" Again, Amma asked them, "My children, don't you have anything to say to Amma?" Again, they all cried out with one voice, "Ammaaaa! Ammaaaa!"

Hearing this expression of love, I understood why Amma's thoughts had been drawn to Amritapuri. The ashram residents were thinking of Amma alone. They did not have any desires or problems to share with her, just desireless, overpowering love. How can God, or the guru, not be attracted by such single-minded love?

For any relationship to flourish, both parties must be attracted to each other. So, the first step is to cultivate our bond with Amma. Then we can take steps to become more attractive to her. We don't do this with makeup or expensive clothes, but with positive inner qualities like kindness, compassion, and selflessness. It is not easy to develop these qualities, but in the presence of a role model like Amma, they begin to awaken almost spontaneously.

Here is an example from my own experience. Many years ago, when the other senior swamis and I were still novice brahmacharis, Amma gave us the job of serving lunch and dinner to the ashram residents. Amma strictly instructed that whoever was serving the food should not eat until everyone else had eaten and the dining hall floor was clean. Only then were we to eat our meal.

For some reason, I did not like this particular job, and I often wondered when Amma would transfer me to another department. Then one day, Amma walked into the dining hall and began serving the food herself. She went directly to where the devotees were seated and moved from person to person, lovingly placing food on each plate. I followed along behind her, serving another dish. When the devotees had finished eating, Amma scrubbed the dining hall floor herself.

The next day, as I was serving food, Amma's example lingered in my mind. Remembering her inspired me to perform the work with sincere enthusiasm and love. Even though that happened many years ago, the memory of that day remains strong in me. To this day, I never miss a chance to serve food.

Allow me to share one more story on this theme. Once long ago, while Amma was giving darshan, she suddenly stopped hugging. Her attention seemed to go elsewhere for a few seconds. Then she said, "The cow is crying." I was surprised to hear her say this. People were loudly singing bhajans, and the cowshed was quite a distance from the temple where darshan was taking place. Nobody else had heard the cow cry. How could Amma have heard it?

Amma immediately stood up and started walking towards the cowshed. When she got there, she found a crying cow who had not been fed or given a bath that day. The little cow was covered in its own dung. Amma called the brahmachari who should have taken care of the cow and asked him for an explanation. The brahmachari admitted that he had overslept and had skipped his duties in the cowshed, so he could attend the morning meditation.

Amma replied, "How would you feel if someone forgot to feed you, or if you had to walk around all day covered in dung without having a bath? Doing your duty sincerely is itself a form of meditation. In fact, attending to the needs of speechless animals, who are not even able to say what they want or need, is more important than meditation."

Amma immediately began to wash and feed the cow. The brahmachari tried to help, but Amma insisted on doing the work herself. This experience made a strong impression on the young man, who had been raised as the apple of his mother's eye and was not used to doing any work at home. After seeing Amma care for the cow, he never again failed to discharge his duties in the cowshed.

Amma ended by telling the brahmachari a story: Once there was a doctor who was devoted to the Divine Mother.

One day during his meditation, She appeared before him. At that moment he heard someone cry out at the entrance of his house. Even though he was dazzled by the vision of the Divine Mother, he got up, ran to the door, and found a wounded man lying on the doorstep.

After he cared for the patient, he returned to the puja room. To his shock, the Divine Mother was still there! He felt terrible that She had waited and apologized profusely to the goddess for leaving Her alone. She replied, "My son, if you had not gone to attend to the needs of that wounded man, I would have disappeared immediately. But because you put his happiness before your own, I was compelled to wait here for you. God will always be with a person who is selflessly serving others."

15—Effort and Grace

Some years ago in Munich, a lady came for Amma's darshan. It was her first time. Because I speak Tamil, the woman's mother tongue, she began to share her problems with me and asked me to tell Amma about them. The woman's husband had recently abandoned her and their children, and she had no job. She lived in another city a few hours away and had taken the train to Munich in hopes that Amma could help her.

After I shared her story with Amma, Amma replied, "Tell her to come back tonight." The lady looked dejected and explained that she had already booked a non-refundable ticket for that afternoon and had no place to stay in Munich. To make matters worse, her children were home alone. No one was watching them.

I explained all this to Amma, but she remained silent. I shrugged my shoulders and said to the lady, "Amma didn't reply. But, if Amma says to come back for the evening program, there's a good reason. You should do it."

To be honest, I didn't expect the woman to come back. But while I was helping with the darshan line, I saw her and told Amma that she had returned. Amma immediately gestured to a man sitting by her side, pointed at the woman, and said, "Son, that lady has no job. Can you help her?"

"Of course, Amma," he replied. "I am happy to give her a job."

There is more to this story than meets the eye. The man, it turns out, was a devotee from the very town the woman lived in. He ran a large business there and had come to Munich that morning for a meeting. After his meeting, on his way back to the airport, he happened to see a poster with Amma's photo and details about her Munich program. He spontaneously decided to go see Amma and rebooked his ticket for the next day.

What's remarkable is this: Amma told the lady to come back for the evening program *before* the businessman had even seen the poster. So how did Amma know the business owner would be at the program that night? This is the nature of Amma's grace.

Amma says that for grace to flow, there must first be at least a little effort on our part. Perhaps Amma asked the woman to return in the evening, had her make that extra effort, so that God's grace could begin to flow.

This reminds me of a lesson in effort and grace that we swamis received back in the 1980s when we were brahmacharis. It was during the pilgrimage to Arunachala Mountain that I mentioned earlier.

The special feature of Tiruvannamalai is that the mountain standing there is the town's temple. Arunachala Mountain is considered to be a manifestation of God Himself. As such, the main practice there is to reverently circumambulate the mountain.

As we drove to Tiruvannamalai for our pilgrimage, we were all brimming with enthusiasm to walk around the mountain. However, once there, we suddenly became very advanced spiritual aspirants and began saying, "Well, Amma is God. Let's just walk around Amma's room. That is just as holy as walking around the mountain." Actually, if that had been our real reason for not walking around the mountain, it would have been perfectly okay. But the truth is, we were just lazy. Amma knew this. So, one morning around 11:00 a.m., seeing us all hanging around her room, Amma suddenly jumped up and started walking. Naturally, we all followed her.

Tiruvannamalai is in a part of Tamil Nadu that is very hot and dry, which is why the *pradakshina* (circumambulation) of the mountain usually starts before sunrise. But Amma chose to start at 11:30 when the heat of the sun was beating down hard.

Soon Amma said, "I'm so thirsty. I need water."

Of course, we were not at all prepared. We had no water. So, we all ran helter-skelter to find some for her. When we came back, Amma drank it all. We walked on for another thirty minutes or so, and Amma said again, "I am so thirsty. More water!"

Again, we ran off to find water.

This happened four times. So, in the end, our pradakshina was very long. When all was said and done, we had walked fourteen miles rather than the seven it normally takes to circumambulate the mountain.

We may say, "Amma is a mahatma! Why did she feel a need to walk around the mountain? Did she do this to resolve some discontentment in herself?" Definitely not! Or we may ask, "Why did Amma need water so badly? Does that mean she was somehow lacking in that moment?" Not at all. By walking around the mountain and repeatedly asking for water, Amma was accomplishing two things at once. She was helping us to transcend our laziness and pushing us to make more effort to purify our minds.

Each and every one of Amma's words and actions are aimed at uplifting us and bringing us closer to God, our True Self. May we all do our part too, by putting in as much effort as we can while the cool breeze of Amma's grace is at our back.

16—Her Example Transforms Us

Amma often says that even though our bodies have grown in height and width, our minds have yet to expand. In many ways, we are still like ten-year-old children. When we look at the world, we see so many things that we would like to change. But when we look at the world inside of us, hardly any of us see things that need to change. Even when we do, we are often too lazy to do anything about it.

Once a man went to his doctor and told him that he could no longer do all the things that he used to do. At the end of the examination, the man bravely said, "Doc, don't worry. Tell me in plain English. What is wrong with me? I can take it."

"In plain English," the doctor replied, "you're just lazy."

"Okay," said the man. "Now give me the medical term, so I can tell my wife."

This story points out one of the most difficult parts of the spiritual journey—being able to see and overcome our old, self-destructive habits. Even when our goals are high, our deeply ingrained patterns of thinking and acting often pull us down.

That's why a living connection with a true spiritual master is so important. Amma helps us rise out of our deep-rooted habits, sometimes without our even realizing it. As Amma often says, tremendous growth takes place just by sitting at the feet of a Realized Master. But this inevitably requires sacrificing the things we're attached to.

Somehow or the other, sacrifice seems to come naturally when we are near Amma. Her programs often go way past our bedtime, yet many of us find ourselves happily sacrificing our beauty sleep to spend more time near Amma. Many of us also find ourselves skipping meals here and there to maximize our time in her presence. While eating and sleeping are essential, in spiritual life it is important to assert control over our body and senses. If we have no control over the whims of the body, we will not be able to sit in meditation for more than a few minutes. In Amma's presence we easily gain such control; this is true spiritual growth. Because of our love for Amma, we find ourselves doing many things we would otherwise not be able to do.

To be honest, when I first joined the ashram, I was not very interested in attending the morning archana. Back then, the starting time was 4:30 a.m., and even though I knew it would be good for my spiritual growth, I often chose to sleep in instead. Then out of the blue, Amma herself began attending archana, and I immediately started participating. I thought, if Amma, who is giving darshan from morning to night, can go for the morning prayers, then surely, I can too!

Back then, there was no set time for Amma's darshan. Day, night, or in the wee hours of the morning, people would just show up, knock on Amma's door, and receive her blessings! Despite this, Amma came to archana every morning without fail. Ultimately, our bond with Amma, our love for her, inspired us to go too. And as a result, we all developed greater physical, mental, and spiritual strength.

When we swamis first joined the ashram, we sometimes got into heated arguments. At first, Amma tried to correct us with reprimands, but we had already read in the scriptures that the anger of a Satguru is just for show. Having read this, we were convinced that Amma was never really mad at us, and so even when she scolded us, it did not have much effect. So Amma tried a different approach. In order to put an end to our arguments, Amma would sometimes give up eating. Seeing Amma torment her own body was unbearable, and so after every argument, we immediately made peace with each other and then did sadhana. Amma knew that punishing us wouldn't really change the situation. But by punishing herself, she created the inner awareness we needed to change our behavior. Knowing that Amma was fasting due to our misbehavior helped us to quickly transcend our pettiness.

It is the same for all of us. By associating with Amma, imbibing her teachings, and putting them into practice, we find that we are often able to see the big picture when trying situations arise. Slowly, we learn to embrace these situations rather than curse them.

Some years ago, I was supposed to go to a country to give a satsang and meditation program. However, as I was going through customs, the officials there began examining my passport in painstaking detail. They started asking questions about me, Amma's organization, and my travels. This went on for about ten minutes. Then, they took me to another room. All the other people sitting there looked like drug dealers and criminals. The officials started asking me more questions. Then someone took my airline ticket and went to make a photocopy of it.

While this was going on, a very tough-looking officer came and took two of the drug dealers away into yet another room. Soon after that, a man came in and asked me to follow him. When he took me to the third room, I became a little worried. I figured it was only a matter of time before the beatings began. But then, this thought came, "I have come here to talk about Amma. If Amma wants me to do that, I will do it. If not, I will just sit here. After all, Amma is the one who has sent me. If I have to go to jail, I will go to jail." At that moment, another officer came in and asked me to follow him. He seemed very serious and sternly led me down a narrow corridor. At the end of the corridor there was a door. He opened the door, extended his arm, and said, "Ok, you can go now."

Even though I was a little nervous at first, ultimately, I was able to transcend most of my tension by remembering that I was there to do Amma's work. Normally, when we run into a negative situation in life, we immediately begin cursing our circumstances, saying things like, "I will never come here again! What was my boss *thinking* when she sent me to this place?" However, no such thoughts entered my mind. I was calm. The feeling in my heart was, "Amma has created this situation. Whatever comes, I will be fine in the end."

Amma always tells us that in truth we are not the doer, but merely the instrument of action, like a pen in the hand of a writer, or a brush in the hand of a painter. When we adopt this attitude, we naturally find that, without any conscious effort on our part, we become more and more accepting of the trials and tribulations that life throws at us. This is yet another way that Amma helps us grow.

Even though Amma has nothing to attain in this world, she continues to work just as tirelessly as she did when she was a young girl. Back then she managed the entire household for her sick mother. Perhaps, in the end, it is Amma's example, her steadfast dedication to helping others, which transforms us most of all.

17—Choosing Our Attitude

Once a man fell out of a second-story window. As he lay there on the ground, a large crowd gathered around him. Seeing the tumult, a police officer walked over and asked, "What happened to you?"

"Don't ask me," the man replied. "I just got here."

Our situation is not so different. We have no idea how we got here, where we came from, and where we are going in life.

Amma says that, like the man in the joke, our lives are a mixture of things we can control and things we can't. For example, we have no control over when we are born, where we are born, or who our parents are. We have no control over how tall we are going to be or what we are going to look like. Such things are completely dictated by our *prarabdha karma* (the result of actions performed in our past lives).

Whether you accept this or not, the real question is: How do you intend to live? Will you live in a manner that benefits you and society, or will you decide to go another way? It all depends on the goals you choose and the decisions you make. This is completely in your hands. In a nutshell, we can decide the values we want to live by.

Once there was a father who had two sons. The father was a drunkard and very abusive. He regularly beat his wife and children and was constantly in and out of jail. When the boys were still young, he left one night and never returned. As time went on, one son became exactly like his father, a criminal and an addict. The other son chose a different path and dedicated his life to selfless service; his goal was to help as many people as he possibly could.

One day the boys' uncle came to visit them. Midway through the conversation, he turned to the first son and asked, "How did you sink so low?" The son responded, "It's all because of dad!

How else could I turn out with a father like him?" The uncle then turned to the second son and asked, "How did you manage to become such a good man?" The second son replied, "It's all because of our father. Every time I saw him get drunk and beat up mom and us kids, I made a firm resolve that I would never become like him."

As this story shows, the circumstances we find ourselves in are not up to us, but how we respond to them is completely in our hands.

Like the boys in this story, Amma was born into challenging circumstances, especially for a spiritual aspirant. Her parents were religious, but not spiritual. As such, she was not given any time for meditation, and there were no gurus or holy people to advise her. Even as a young girl, Amma was expected to work from 4:00 a.m. until almost midnight every single day.

Despite all of this, Amma took the circumstances she was given and made the very best of them. She saw all of her chores and responsibilities as gifts given to her directly from God. In this way, everything Amma did became spiritual practice, a way of worshipping the Lord. This was true whether she was gathering food for the cows and goats, scrubbing the pots and pans, or hand-washing the family's laundry.

But this attitude of worship was not confined to her chores. Amma chose to look upon all the people she interacted with as divine too. When collecting fodder for the cows from her neighbors, she would often come across old and sick people. Looking upon them as embodiments of the Lord Himself, Amma would stop what she was doing to give them hot baths, wash their clothes, and feed them with her own hands. Amma never ran away from work; she embraced it as divine. When our goal in life is firm, we will persevere no matter what.

Even after Amma started giving darshan, challenges persisted. Aiming to put an end to Amma's darshan, some people in the village formed a so-called 'Rationalist Movement,' claiming that Amma was a fraud. For a time, it seemed everyone was against Amma, even her own family. But Amma's mind was strong, mature, and resilient, and so none of these criticisms affected her. In the end, many of the rationalists realized that none of their efforts to stop Amma's darshan were having any effect at all. Instead, they found their own lives becoming increasingly difficult. Eventually they came to see that Amma's approach to life led to happiness and success, while their approach led to frustration and failure. Thus, many so-called Rationalists eventually realized that Amma's way was far more rational than theirs. Some even became Amma's devotees.

Amma's life is her message. It provides a perfect example of how we can attain our goals in life, no matter how difficult the external circumstances. With determination and God's grace, we can even attain the ultimate goal of life.

18—Shifting Our Perspective

When former President Barack Obama was running for office, the American people really seemed to respond to his campaign slogan, "Change We Can Believe In." Change became a very hot word during that election campaign. It was contagious. As election day approached, even the incumbent party began talking about the need for change. In response, Obama's campaign changed their slogan to "The Change We Need." Though not everyone agreed on what kind of change was needed, everyone agreed change itself was essential.

Humankind has been seeking change since the beginning of time with all kinds of economic, social, and political strategies. There have been revolutions and wars. New political parties have come and gone. New laws, bills, and constitutions have been drafted. Against this backdrop, Amma consistently reminds us that real, permanent change does not come by merely transforming external factors. *Real* change, Amma says, will only come when we transform our minds—our way of thinking, seeing, and responding to the world around us. Ironically, these days everyone wants others to change first. It is hard to find people who sincerely understand that they themselves need to change. But unless transformation takes place in people's inner world, nothing will truly change in the outer world.

Once, as a ship captain was inspecting his sailors, he turned to the men and said, "You smell bad! Men, you need to be cleaner. From now on, please be sure to regularly change your socks and underwear!"

"Aye! Aye! Captain!" the men shouted back in unison.

But when the next inspection rolled around, they all smelled just as bad. The surprised captain said, "I thought I told you guys to change your socks and underwear!"

The first mate stepped forward and said, "Aye, aye, sir! We did, sir! Jim changed with Dan; Jeff changed with Rodney; and Phillip changed with Derrick."

Like these sailors, many people do try to change things in their lives. They may try a new hairstyle, hair color, or brand of clothes, but somehow, they remain dissatisfied. Compare this with Amma. She inhabits the same world you and I live in, yet everywhere Amma looks she sees beauty. This is because Amma has realized the ultimate truth that everything is a manifestation of the Divine. As such, her love flows out to one and all—to all people, animals, mountains, trees, and rivers. Where there is love, there can only be beauty and bliss, never ugliness. Where there is love, all of life becomes a celebration, a wonderful story in which everyone plays their part. As spiritual aspirants, it is this kind of inner change we are after, a change in perspective, a change in vision.

The role of a Satguru like Amma is to help bring about this change. In the *Guru Gita*, a collection of verses in praise of the Guru, one verse says:

ajñāna-timirāndhasya jñānāñjana-śalākayā |
cakṣur unmīlitaṁ yena tasmai śrī-gurave namaḥ ||

Salutations to that guru who opened the eyes of one blind due to the cataract of ignorance with a needle coated with the ointment of knowledge.

Amma is the great spiritual ophthalmologist who, out of compassion, has come to help us change how we see God, ourselves, the world, and other people. When she changes how we see, it's not like replacing green-tinted lenses with pink ones. That's not what the guru does. Amma's role is to remove all of the tinting—be it blue, black, or pink. Her job is to help us see the blissful reality, the way things truly are. The guru removes the cataracts of ignorance, and our job is to lie still and let Dr. Amma do her work.

Amma changes our vision in two important ways: She changes how we see ourselves and how we see others.

Honestly, most of us have no idea who we truly are. If asked about ourselves, we're likely to recite a list of facts: our name, age, gender, profession, and academic degrees. We may go on to mention our spouse, our children and their ages, genders, education, and accomplishments. Then we might start talking about things we love, like Ben & Jerry's Ice Cream and Pizza Hut. Of course, then we will go on to discuss the things we don't like… rainy days, our boss, our next-door neighbor.

But the guru wants us to go deeper, to see beyond the superficial. She wants us to understand that we are not the body, mind, or intellect; that we are not our likes and dislikes; that we are pure, blissful consciousness, ever-shining. As this understanding deepens, we gain tremendous strength to face the difficulties and tribulations that come our way.

One day, a man walked out of a store and saw a traffic officer busy writing a parking ticket. The man went up to the officer and said, "How about giving a guy a break?" The officer ignored him and continued writing the ticket. "Why do you have to be such a jerk?" the man asked. The officer glared at him but remained silent, then began writing a second ticket for bald tires. Despite this, the man continued to challenge the officer. After finishing the second ticket, the officer proceeded to write yet another ticket—this time for a faulty windshield wiper. This went on for about twenty minutes. The more the man challenged the officer, the more tickets the officer wrote. After writing several tickets, the officer left.

A passerby who saw the whole thing approached the man and asked, "Why did you do that?"

"Well, it doesn't really affect me," replied the man. "My car is parked around the corner."

Because the man knew that the car wasn't his, the parking tickets had no effect on him at all. Similarly, when we understand that our body and mind are not our True Self, that we are the Atma, no adversity will be able to touch us. Challenging situations will be just like someone writing tickets for a car that does not belong to us. This shift in perspective is "the change we need." The point of the story is not that we should create trouble for others, but that we should move through life unaffected by its ups and downs, like butter floating on water.

And yet, changing how we see ourselves is not enough. We also need to change how we see others. Currently, our fellow human beings seem separate from us; we see them as 'other.' But Amma says that we are not separate entities, that we are connected like the links of a chain. As we begin to change our vision, and start seeing others as our brothers and sisters, a deep sense of unity and compassion arises, which, in turn, affects the way we feel about the world and act in it.

Along these lines, I am reminded of a touching scene that took place during a recent darshan. Amma was embracing a huge crowd. In fact, Amma had been giving darshan like this all week, starting around 10 a.m. and continuing late into the night, often until three or four the next morning. Out of concern for her, an American devotee approached her and said, "Amma, why can't you take a vacation? Maybe you could go to Hawaii and relax on the beach. We devotees would pay for it, and you could rest your body."

Amma laughed at the man's innocence and replied with a smile, "You have a son, right? If he were sick, or sad, or needed you, would you be able to just take off and go to the beach? Of course not! You would stay with him. This is how it is with

Amma. All are my children, and I cannot leave them just to take a vacation."

If we are to truly change our world, we must embrace Amma's perspective and learn to see each person we encounter as a beloved member of our family. If we can make this shift, we will be happy no matter what, whether we're in heaven or in hell. When someone transforms this way, their outer life virtually always follows suit. The very presence of such a person transforms the world around them for the better.

Suppose someone in our workplace falls in love. We quickly notice that his whole mood changes. He walks into the office beaming and smiling at everyone. Even if the boss yells at him, he isn't affected. Seeing his joy, we feel uplifted too. The whole atmosphere in the office changes, and when we go home, we treat our family members with more love, and on and on it goes.

With this in mind, we realize there is no way to calculate just how much Amma has transformed the world through her darshan. Her interactions with people, her very presence, have created a tremendous positive vibration within them, setting off an immense chain-reaction. As the following story illustrates, when we start following Amma's teachings by meditating, doing *mantra japa*, and introspecting, we change for the better, and the world around us changes too.

Not long after the 2004 Tsunami, a couple came to visit their son who lived in Amritapuri. They spent a week or so at the ashram and then stopped off at a five-star resort for three days. The difference they saw between the opulent resort and the humble self-sacrifice at Amma's ashram hit them square in the heart. Seeing these two totally different environments side by side helped them to understand that Amma was guiding people towards selflessness to uplift the world. It was equally clear to them that most of the world was laser-focused on the exact opposite—pleasure and comfort alone. Inspired, the couple wired their son a large sum of money, the same amount they had spent on their five-star hotel, and asked him to donate it to Amma's charities.

Amma's darshan impacts everyone. Some are struck by its power immediately, while others respond a bit more slowly. Either way, Amma's physical touch always leads to inner spiritual transformation.

We honor this gift of transformation when we choose to bring her presence into our daily lives. We can do this in any situation by asking, "What would Amma do?" Tuning into that and following through with action is a practical way to share her presence with others. If we practice this consistently, it is sure to refine our hearts and minds.

Some years ago, I was overseas for a program. On the way to the airport, I happened to notice a pile of trash and some empty bottles lying next to a building. I was a bit surprised because that country is generally so clean. Anyway, I kept on walking until this question came to mind: "What would Amma have done if she had seen that trash?" She would have cleaned it up! So, I found a small plastic bag, returned to the building, picked up the bottles, and put them in the trash.

If we can remember to ask what Amma would do when challenges arise in our family and work lives, it will be just like living with Amma all the time. It will help us to cultivate the focused awareness that is essential for spiritual growth. And the world will benefit too.

You might say it is a small thing to pick up some trash. But Amma has given darshan to millions of people, and her influence has touched each one of them. What if these millions chose to pick up trash every single time they saw it lying on the ground? What would the world look like?

During Obama's acceptance speech in Chicago, he continued with the theme of change saying, "This victory alone is not the change we seek. It is only the chance for us to make that change." This is true in our life with Amma as well. We have all found Amma. She has come into our lives. But just meeting Amma, or having her darshan, is not enough on its own. If we truly want to change, we need to take Amma's teachings to heart and put them into practice each day. Why not start now?

19—Her Advice Never Fails

One day a man was walking past the city courthouse when he spotted a friend sitting on the steps outside. His friend was sobbing loudly with his head buried in his hands.

"What's the matter?" the man asked. "Did your lawyer give you bad advice?"

The friend looked up and said, "No, it's worse than that. He didn't give it to me. He *sold* it to me."

Advice is easy to come by in life, but good advice is rare. Even rarer is free good advice.

Often in life, the path is obvious. We don't even have to think about it. We just keep moving forward. But occasionally, we are at a total loss. We find ourselves in situations where we have two or three options but just don't know what to do. As we just discussed, when making such decisions, asking ourselves what Amma would do is a good guide.

But occasionally, even this doesn't work. As the scriptures say, sometimes dharma can be extremely subtle and difficult to discern. In such moments, we may turn to friends or paid professionals to help us make our decision. Sometimes their advice works out, and sometimes it doesn't.

That is why we are all so fortunate. We have the most precious source of guidance possible — Amma. If we allow ourselves to be guided by her, we can rest assured that we are walking the dharmic path.

This is what our scriptures say:

ye tatra brāhmaṇāḥ saṃmarśinaḥ. yuktā āyuktāḥ. alūkṣā.
dharmakāmāḥ syuḥ yathā te tatra varteran. tathā tatra
vartethāḥ ||

Taittiriya Upanishad 1.11.4

If any confusion arises regarding one's conduct, or dharma, one should follow the example of those mahatmas of good judgment, dedicated to dharma, who are united with the *Atman*, who are not controlled by others, and who are ever compassionate.

In short, we will never go wrong if we follow the advice and example of mahatmas like Amma. In fact, the Upanishads counsel us to follow their advice to the letter because mahatmas embody five qualities that make their every word perfect: *sammarsinah* (good judgement), *yuktah* (unity with the Atman), *ayuktah* (impartiality), *dharma-kamaha* (dedication to dharma), and *aluksha* (compassion).

The first quality all Mahatmas possess is good judgement. They are deep thinkers imbued with subtle, expansive thinking. They can see every single facet of the problems we share with them.

Let me share an example of this.

Once, when Amma was in Europe, a man with three daughters came for darshan. Though he had once had a good job, he lost it. Now he couldn't even pay his rent. To make matters worse, he had to take his children out of school because he could no longer afford the fees. With the small unemployment check he was receiving, he could only afford to buy them food. After his darshan, he came to the side of Amma's chair and explained his problem to me. He ended by saying, "Swamiji, to be honest, I really want to have a son."

'What a strange person!' I thought to myself. 'He cannot even afford to properly feed and educate his three daughters. Why in the world does he want to have another child?' So, I said, "It sounds like you're already in dire straits. How will you support another baby?"

At that very moment, Amma turned to me and asked, "What are you two talking about?"

"Amma," I replied, "he had a question, so I was answering it."

"Is the question for you or for me?" she asked.

"It's for you, Amma," I replied.

Amma looked confused and asked, "Then why are you answering it?"

"Amma," I replied, "it was such an easy question. I did not want to bother you with it."

I went on to explain the man's problems to Amma. Without missing a beat, Amma enthusiastically gave him completely different advice: "Don't worry, my son. Amma will help you. You will have a baby boy."

I reluctantly translated Amma's response. To me, it seemed almost as surprising as the question itself. The man left satisfied and happy, while I stood there totally bewildered.

Two years later, the man returned for darshan, bouncing a baby boy in his arms. Seeing the baby, I thought, 'Oh, no! Now he must really be struggling!' But I would only get the real story when he came up for darshan.

When it was his turn, he profusely thanked Amma for his baby boy and added that he had a nice job now. I was shocked. After he left, Amma explained everything. She told me that because of his strong, unfulfilled desire for a baby boy, he had become totally depressed and could not focus on his work. Finally, he stopped going to work altogether and lost his job. But once Amma fulfilled his desire for a son, he regained the enthusiasm that depression had stolen from him. That's why he was able to get a good job again, and everything returned to normal.

This story shows the tremendous depth of Amma's perspective in every situation. Though her answer consisted of just a few words, behind those words was a powerful resolve that removed all his problems. All too often, we fail to recognize the infinite power and wisdom concealed in Amma's five-foot-tall body.

The second quality that makes Amma the perfect guide is yukta. Because Amma is united with the Atman, she fully understands what is righteous and what is not in every situation. Her clarity comes from her total lack of self-interest and the absence of ego. Not only does Amma see with penetrating and expansive vision, but she also knows what is dharmic and what is not—even when the line may seem blurry to us.

Let me give a practical example. Sometimes we see someone begging, and we want to help him. But we can't figure out what to give or how much. These things are not always so clear. The person could be a drug addict or an alcoholic, and the money could go to support those vices. Someone like Amma is able to see into the heart of each situation and know what is proper and what is not.

As the following story shows, the people we usually go to for advice lack this kind of clear thinking.

Once a bachelor was having money problems. He couldn't make ends meet and was struggling to pay his rent and put food on the table. Nothing was going his way. So, he decided to ask a friend for advice.

His friend said, "I have a 100% foolproof way to solve your problem for twenty to twenty-five years!"

"Wow! What is that?"

"Rob a bank," his friend replied.

The bachelor was irritated. "What a stupid idea!" he said. "Sure, if it works, I'll be rolling in money. But if I get caught, it'll be a mess! How can you say that is foolproof?"

His friend replied, "If you get away with it, you'll have all the money you need for food and rent. And, if you get caught, you'll get food and rent courtesy of the Federal Government for decades!"

Mahatmas are incapable of giving dodgy advice like this. Their advice is always rooted in righteousness and steeped in wisdom.

The third quality mahatmas like Amma possess is impartiality. They are not under anyone's thumb. As a result, they can be 100% impartial in all their dealings and actions. They have no biases or family ties to bind them. They are not in the pocket of any government, political organization, or social group. They are not even limited by religion.

If you look at Amma's wide array of charitable humanitarian programs—the millions of sick people who have received free healthcare, the 47,000 homeless who have received homes, the thousands of scholarships, the millions of dollars spent on natural-disaster relief—all of it is given to deserving people no matter what their caste, creed, or religion. Getting advice from Amma is not like getting advice from, say, a scientist who is in the pocket of a big corporation. Amma has no biases. This is why her closing prayer is always the same: *om lokah samastah sukhino bhavantu*— "May everyone everywhere be happy and peaceful."

The fourth quality that makes Amma's advice perfect is devotion to dharma, which is closely connected with impartiality. In essence, it means that Amma only has one bias: the desire that dharma be done. She desires that people do what is good and righteous. Why? Because it is only when we treat others with love, respect, and honesty that individuals and society can flourish and progress.

The final quality that makes Amma's advice unsurpassable is compassion. We can always trust Amma's advice because she is compassionate by nature. Compassion is the very reason Amma sings bhajans, delivers satsang, and gives darshan. Feeling our pain as her own, Amma has dedicated her life to being there for us—to hearing our sorrows and wiping away our tears. Amma often reminds us that we all have compassion deep inside of us. It is intrinsic, but we need to awaken it. Amma is here to help us do just that.

Let me share a story that highlights the subtlety of Amma's compassion. Some time ago, a devotee came to ask Amma a question. The devotee said that she was moving to another country, but there was a big problem. For the last year or so, she had been feeding a wild cat that lived in the forest near her home. Each day the cat would come to her house, and she would give it some milk and food. "Amma," she said, "I'm afraid the cat has become dependent on me. If I move, what will it do for food? Should I take it with me?"

I thought to myself, "Of course, you should take the cat. Why ask this?"

But Amma saw it differently. "Daughter," she replied. "That cat may have a wife and children in the forest. If you take him, he will miss them so much, and they will miss him. You should leave him where he is. He will be okay. I appreciate your love and compassion toward the cat, but our compassion should never harm others and should be rooted in knowledge."

The lady immediately understood and said, "Thank you, Amma. I will leave the cat where it is."

Amma saw with both subtlety and expansiveness. Subtly, Amma looked into the difficulties that arise when a wild cat becomes dependent on a human for food. But she also looked beyond and could see the cat's ability to readjust. Not only that, Amma was able to look into the cat's family life and see how his absence would damage his family. And, of course, Amma looked deeply into the mind-set of the devotee as well. On the surface, Amma saw the compassion in the devotee's mind, but she also saw that, on a deeper level, the devotee was developing attachment to the cat. It was only after weighing all these factors that Amma gave her advice. This is why Amma finally said to the lady, "Our compassion should never harm others."

The interesting thing about these five qualities is that just one is not enough. We need all of them when making choices. Otherwise, our decisions will be unbalanced.

Amma likes to tell a story about one of her attendants, who is full of compassion. It goes like this. Once an elderly devotee was going up the stairs to Amma's room. He was disabled and had to walk with crutches. Seeing him struggle to get up the steps, Amma's attendant was flooded with compassion. She decided to help him. Do you know what she did? She began taking away his crutches, so she could carry them for him! Of course, when she removed his first crutch, he started to fall. Luckily, we were there to catch him.

We are all incredibly blessed to have Amma as our role model. But ultimately, Amma wants us to develop all five of these qualities ourselves. She wants us to become deep thinkers, who understand the subtlety of dharma, who desire righteousness, who are unbiased, who are compassionate. As we develop these qualities, we will eventually become completely independent. This is the path Amma is guiding us along, the path from dependence to independence. With Amma's help, we are on a journey to awaken our own inner power and talents for the benefit of the world.

20—Master Your Mind and Be Happy

Recently in an interview, a journalist began listing some of Amma's accomplishments to her. "Amma," he said, "you are a world-recognized humanitarian, a spiritual leader, the chancellor of a leading university, the founder of a medical-care system that has provided totally free care to more than three million people. You have spoken at the United Nations, the Parliament of World Religions, and the Vatican ... And, yet, you come from a poor fishing village and have had only a few years of formal education. Do you find it wondrous that you came from nothing to all of this?"

Amma's answer was illuminating. She said, "I don't give any value to such attainments. If you see this as a wonder, then what about the huge banyan tree coming from just a tiny seed? Don't you consider that a wonder? To me, the real wonder would be if all of mankind were to become happy."

The first thing that shines through in Amma's response is her absolute humility, and there are two other important takeaways. First, Mahatmas like Amma do not view outer accomplishments as a big deal. To them, such accomplishments are insignificant. Someone like Amma comes into this world with full Self-knowledge, chooses exactly where she wants to be born, who her parents will be, what her circumstances will be, and what qualities she will need to accomplish her mission. So, as miraculous as these accomplishments may seem to us, from the mahatma's perspective, they are just like a seed becoming the tree it is destined to be.

Second, for a Mahatma, the real wonder is when a person becomes permanently happy. Thus, the greatest miracle for Amma would be for the entire world to become happy, rooted in their true Self.

This happiness will only dawn if we learn to discipline our minds. The Buddha put it this way: "Your worst enemy cannot harm you as much as your own unguarded thoughts. On the other hand, once mastered, no one can help you as much." Long before Buddha, Sri Krishna said the same thing:

> *"Let a person raise himself by his own self. Let him not debase himself. For he himself is his greatest friend and greatest foe."*
> (*Bhagavad Gita* 6:5)

If our mind is not under our control, or "a friend" as the Buddha says, it will never become happy. Even in the presence of a mahatma like Amma, who radiates inner peace, we will not be happy until our minds are under our control.

Thus, discipline is the one spiritual practice that we can never abandon. Whether we consider ourselves a spiritual novice or a seasoned veteran, we must develop the quality of discipline, along with universal values like compassion, patience, and truthfulness. For if our minds remain unrefined, no matter how great our guru is, no matter how much time she spends explaining our true nature to us, that knowledge will not bear fruit.

Self-knowledge is different from all other types of knowledge. As a seer once said, "One cannot just 'do' Self-knowledge the way one 'does' mathematics or history. Unless our lifestyle and value system are in harmony with the demands of the Truth we are pursuing, we can never hope for real enlightenment." For the bud of our hearts to blossom into Self-realization, we must first cultivate human values in our lives.

21—Good Samskaras for a Happy Life

These days, most people do not have to hunt for food, build fires for warmth, or struggle to find shelter. In fact, cutting-edge technology allows us to complete our daily tasks more quickly than ever, giving us more free time. Despite this, we are far behind our ancestors in at least one important respect: *samskaras* (spiritual culture and values). And because of this lack of values, we often end up wasting the free time we have.

Once a man landed a job in a factory loading bags of vegetables onto a truck. On his very first day on the job, his supervisor noticed a problem. While all the other workers were carrying two bags at a time, the new worker was carrying only one. When the supervisor asked the worker why this was, he boasted, "I am not as lazy as those other fellows. They are unwilling to make two trips!"

Like the man in the story, without the spiritual value of discrimination, we will not be able to make the best use of our time. Of course, there is nothing wrong with having fun, but without samskara, we will soon find that worldly pleasures begin to lose their flavor. When we engage in entertainment devoid of samskara, our mental peace begins to dissolve to the point that even the smallest of problems, like traffic jams, can ruin our day.

Once a young vacationing couple were driving through the countryside. They had just had an argument and were traveling in sullen silence. Finally, as they passed a barnyard filled with mules and pigs, the husband sarcastically asked, "Are they relatives of yours?"

"Yes," the wife replied. "I married into the family."

Though the young couple had intended to spend the day relaxing, they were not able to adjust to each other and ended up wasting their free time in misery.

When we go to an amusement park, carnival, or shopping mall, we encounter many attractive sights that create desires in us. The result is that our downtime ends up making us restless rather than relaxed. Without culture, we will misuse the free time allotted to us and spoil ourselves and sometimes others as well. To enjoy our free time properly, we must have spiritual culture and values.

Free time can be a double-edged sword, for when we have free time, we have to deal with ourselves. In fact, many people find it difficult to be alone even for a short time. That's why we are given music to listen to when we are put on hold during customer service calls. As soon as we are alone and unoccupied, we become aware of thoughts and feelings like anger, inferiority, and jealousy. These unpleasant feelings cause restlessness, and so we grasp for any sound, sight, or sensation that might take our mind off our inner world. These days, most people can't bear even a few minutes of silence and stillness.

All negative thoughts and emotions arise out of our likes and dislikes. In a cultured mind, however, attachment to them is not as strong: the mind is calmer. And, when the mind is still, we can use our free time to simply relax and enjoy the peace within. Or we can even use our free time to decrease our desires by contemplating spiritual principles.

There is a saying, "A rose by any other name is still a rose." But this isn't necessarily true. If four different people look at a rose, they may see four different things. A scientist may think of its Latin name, *rosa*. A devotee may think of offering it to the Lord. A lover may think of offering it to their beloved. And a jilted lover might think of stomping it into the ground. So, while all four may be looking at the same rose, their experience of it may be totally different. In the same way, how we spend our free time will vary greatly depending on the quality of our thoughts. You can tell a lot about a person's level of culture by looking at what they do with their free time.

People tend to fall into one of three categories of cultural refinement: *prakriti* (self-centered), *vikriti* (brashly selfish), and *samskriti* (selfless). If we were to give someone a loaf of bread, he would inevitably act according to one of these three qualities. The person under the sway of prakriti would simply eat the bread. The one influenced by samskriti would share the bread with others before eating it himself. And the one under the thrall of vikriti? Well, he would eat whatever he was given, then take others' share as well.

Amma says that we are meant to rise from prakriti to samskriti, from thinking primarily about ourselves to selflessly helping others. Unfortunately, in today's world, many human beings seem to be doing just the opposite and descending from prakriti to vikriti, from just looking out for "number one" to selfishly taking advantage of others for their own gain.

Nowadays many people, especially youngsters, spend their time playing video games, which benefit neither themselves nor anyone else. Recently, when a new video game system was released in the United States, two customers argued over the last remaining game system in the store. In the end, one of the customers shot and killed the other, so he could have the system for himself.

This is an extreme case. Nonetheless, we should all examine our own lives and look at what we do with our free time. Then we can ask ourselves these questions: Am I at the prakriti level? Do I simply eat, sleep, and take for myself? Or have I sunk to the level of vikriti, taking away from others for my own enjoyment? Finally, we should decide what practical steps we can take to rise to the level of samskriti and start using our free time to uplift ourselves and others.

Most animals simply fall asleep after eating. Cows, however, spend a long time chewing their cud. Amma suggests we do the same—that we digest the events of each day through quiet reflection and journaling. We can ask ourselves: Did I do anything good for others today? Did I hurt anyone with my words or actions? Did I waste time, or use it well? And if we recognize a mistake, we should make a sincere, clear resolve not to repeat it. This kind of daily reflection will help us use our time more and more selflessly.

Amma, of course, has no free time to speak of, so we cannot really talk about what she does with her free time. But in the early days, when Amma was a young girl, she used to ride in a hand-poled boat across the backwaters to do errands for her family. During these boat rides, she was free. Feeling the breeze against her arms, she would experience it as the Divine Mother's caresses. Seeing the small waves in the backwaters, she would see them as the Divine Mother's fluttering sari, or as the Divine Mother dancing. With this image in mind, she would bend down and kiss the waves. Seeing a fish jumping out of the water, Amma would lose herself in ecstasy, reveling in nature's beauty.

And if we were to try to test Amma's level of culture with the bread test, the results would be off the charts. Amma says a samskriti will first share what he has with others before taking anything for himself. But Amma takes this to an entirely different level. On the days that Amma does not give darshan because she is traveling, she refuses to eat. For Amma, just sharing what she has is not enough. She feels that she should first work for others before taking anything for herself.

But what do we do when we get a five-minute break? Maybe we eat something or start flipping through our phone to find a friend to chat with. We might choose to have a cigarette, or chew some gum. Whatever it is, we will probably be using our mouth in some way. The truth is, we could be spending that time helping someone. We could be remembering God.

Earlier in the book, I described how Amma went on a pilgrimage to Tiruvannamalai to fulfill the wishes of some of the brahmacharis. On the first day, as usual, we rose before dawn and performed our morning prayers and meditation. Amma then took us to visit the temple and the top of the mountain. When we returned to the house where we were staying, she went to her room, leaving us to our own devices. We were all tired from our trek up the mountain.

After a good meal, we spent the afternoon chatting and resting. The thought of doing spiritual practices didn't even cross our minds. That night, after the evening bhajans, Amma asked us how we had spent our time that day. As we had not done anything worthwhile, we gave long, evasive answers. After hearing our reply, Amma went to her room, without speaking a word.

The next morning, we got up early. Normally, we would take a bath right away. According to tradition, aspirants should take a bath before beginning their morning prayers. But out of laziness, a few of us resisted taking this cold bath. Though it was actually not very cold outside, we somehow convinced ourselves it was absolutely freezing.

Just then, we heard someone shout that Amma had left her room. We looked outside and saw Amma walking toward the road with Swami Paramatmananda at her side. He looked back at us and called out, "Amma is going to circumambulate the mountain." Even though some of us had been feeling lazy just moments before, when we found out Amma was on the move, we quickly took a cold shower and ran after her.

On her way around the mountain, Amma stopped before every shrine and cave and asked us to chant, "Om" three times. In some places, she asked us to sit and meditate. It usually takes about an hour and a half to walk around the mountain; that day it took us six hours. We spent the rest of that day sitting in meditation and singing bhajans.

Of course, Amma did not circumambulate the mountain for her own sake. She did it for us. Amma confirmed this later, saying that if she had not come out that morning, we would all have wasted the second day of the trip as well. Amma was showing us the proper way to use our time by literally walking the talk. She was instilling good samskaras in us.

May we all transform our free time into quality moments, enriched by human values, remembering that true spiritual growth begins with surrender to a Satguru like Amma. Through such surrender, may our day-to-day actions become grace-filled spiritual practice.

22—Yoga Is Skill in Action

In a well-known verse from the *Bhagavad Gita*, Sri Krishna defines *yoga* this way — *yogah karmasu kausalam*: "Yoga is skill in action." The skill he refers to here can manifest on two levels. On the day-to-day level, it means performing each action efficiently, with grace and skill. On a higher level, it means keeping our mind fixed on the divine, even while engaged in intense, complex actions. The ability to do this is true spiritual attainment. Amma is fully established in this state, which is why her actions are graceful, skillful, and perfect no matter how much she multitasks.

There are countless examples of Amma's skill in action. I will share just one. A few years ago, Amma visited a North Indian city to give darshan there for the first time. Most of the people hosting Amma had never met her before, so they weren't really devotees yet. Even the owner of the house where Amma was staying had never met her before. Nevertheless, the host invited fifty of his closest friends over before the evening program to have an unannounced, private darshan with her. To ensure that Amma could not escape without blessing them, the guests crowded on the staircase outside her room.

As time went on, the crowd became a bit unruly. They were tired of waiting and were worried that Amma would somehow sneak out without seeing them. Their demands were clear: One way or the other they were going to have Amma's darshan.

When word came that Amma was leaving for the program, they refused to budge. They wouldn't move an inch, not even to make space for Amma to walk down the stairs. We were all afraid that Amma might get hurt. To our horror, when Amma smilingly emerged from her room, the people on the staircase rushed towards her. Despite the chaos, Amma didn't shy away from anyone. Instead, she smiled broadly and moved *into the* crowd, drawing each person in for an embrace as she moved forward.

Ten minutes later she was in the car riding down the road towards the program hall. Amma, of course, was completely fine, but a couple of her brahmacharis didn't fare so well. Somehow or other they lost their *dhotis* in the melee.

Later that night, one of us apologized to Amma for the behavior of the crowd. Amma replied with one word — *prema* (Divine Love). This was Amma's one-word commentary on their behavior. We had gotten all wrapped up in the riot, but Amma, as always, was established in the divine Truth at its core.

This is the great challenge we all face in spiritual life: not getting lost in the periphery. Actually, God should become like the theme music to our life, the song that is always playing in the back of our heads, even as we perform our worldly duties.

Once many years ago, while we were sitting by the backwaters, a devotee asked if it was really possible to remember God all the time. Amma responded by pointing to a man in a small canoe who was leading some ducks down the river. "See that small boat?" she asked. "Even though it is so tiny, the boatman is standing in the center, balancing as he rows with that long oar. He does both things at the same time. If any of the ducks stray, he leads them back on course by slapping the water with his oar. Every now and again, he smokes a cigarette. When necessary, he uses his feet to scoop out any water that has splashed into the boat. At times, he chats with the people standing on the riverbank. And yet, while doing all these things, his mind always remains on the boat. If his attention wavers for even a moment, he will lose his balance, the canoe will capsize, and he will fall into the water. Children, we should live in this world like that boatman. Whatever work we are doing, our mind should be centered on God. This is easily possible through practice."

Real skill in action is the ability to remain focused on the divine truth while engaged in action. The mind of a Self-realized soul is like this. He realizes that 'I,' the world, and God are all one and the same divinity. The Enlightened One's mind ever resides in that state of peaceful equilibrium even when engaged in action.

In their innocence, some people worry about Amma's ability to handle the constant flow of devotees. In fact, a few years ago, a devotee confided in Amma, "With all the devotees coming to you and praying to you, I worry that the line will be busy when I really need to reach you."

Amma replied, "Don't worry, my daughter. Amma has a dedicated phone line for each and every one of her children. No one else can use your line." Although this may sound reassuring, we may still doubt this fact, like the man in the following story.

Once a businessman, who needed millions of dollars to land a deal, went to a Sri Lakshmi temple to pray for money. By chance, he found himself standing next to a man who was praying very loudly for $100 to pay an urgent debt. "Oh, Devi!" the man pleaded, "Please, just give me $100! Just $100. Nothing more, nothing less. Please... please... please... Please give me $100!"

The businessman, who couldn't help but hear the man's prayers, walked over to him and pressed a $100 bill into his hand. Overjoyed, the man got up and left the temple. The businessman then closed his eyes and prayed, "Okay, Devi, now that he's gone, and I have your undivided attention, would you please ..."

But this is not how it works with a mahatma like Amma, who has realized her oneness with the omnipresence, omnipotence, and omniscience of God. This is why she can listen to millions of prayers at the same time. Seeing the One in the many, and the many in the One, Amma is able to understand all of our hearts and hear all of our prayers, no matter how many people come to her.

In fact, just last year, Amma said to a devotee, "Tell me, how many hairs are there on your body? Thousands, right? But if I pluck even one, you'll feel it immediately and know exactly where it is. That's how it is for Amma with her millions of children. She's always aware of what's happening in each one's heart."

But becoming more like Amma isn't about mastering the art of multitasking. It's about recognizing the divine presence in all we see, hear, and touch. When we begin to see God in everything, each moment becomes sacred.

We can nurture this divine perspective by asking ourselves each day, "Am I doing enough to ease the suffering of those around me? Could I spend a few more minutes in daily practice? Could I reflect more on Amma's teachings and live them more fully?"

The more we remember that God is present in all, the more lovingly and skillfully we will act. Over time, may we learn to serve like her, speak like her, and love like her with perfect awareness in each moment.

23—Knowledge Must Be Lived

In 2010 SUNY (State University of New York) bestowed a doctorate in humane letters on Amma. But this was not Amma's first degree. Long, long ago, Amma earned a different type of doctorate in happiness. If you want to learn calculus, you go to someone with a PhD in mathematics. If you want to study Shakespeare, you go to someone with a PhD in English Literature. But if you want to learn about happiness—what it is, where it comes from, how to attain it, how *not* to lose it, how to realize it as your own nature—you have to go to someone with a doctorate in happiness. That someone is Amma.

Actually, happiness is not the right word. A better word is bliss. But even that word is limited, just a pointer that indicates something totally beyond. In India we have our own term for someone with a doctorate in happiness, *Atma jnani* (a knower of the Self). This term points to the pinnacle of spiritual attainment. It is the degree that all spiritual aspirants are seeking.

There are two stages in attaining an Atma jnanam degree. The first stage is to attain a basic intellectual understanding of spiritual principles. The second is to fully assimilate those principles and integrate them in your thoughts, words, and deeds. If you have known Amma for several years, attended her programs, listened to her satsangs, and studied her teachings, you may have reached the first level. But the second level is something we are all still striving for. This is why Amma repeatedly says, "What we lack is not spiritual book knowledge but awareness."

What Amma means is that although most of us can understand Vedanta intellectually, we forget these spiritual truths in the hustle and bustle of life. Knowledge is extremely powerful, but forgotten knowledge is just like having no knowledge at all. Most of us intellectually understand that we are not the body. However, when the body experiences pain, we forget this truth and start crying. Most of us intellectually understand that we are not our emotions, but when someone wrongs us, we completely identify with our anger and lose our temper. Most of us understand that the center of who we are is beyond the ideas popping in and out of our head, but how good are we at maintaining this awareness throughout the day? This is why Amma keeps urging us to develop awareness.

Let me share a real-life example. There is a devotee who received a spiritual name from Amma. She had been living in Amma's ashram for several years and had studied the scriptures. The name Amma gave her is very Vedantic. I don't want to use her real name, so let's just call her Sarvavyapini, which means, 'The All-Pervasive One.' She was very happy with her new name, which pointed toward the true nature of the Self.

One day, Amma decided to name another devotee Sarvavyapini. When the original Sarvavyapini came to know about this, she became very upset. She stormed up to Amma full of anger and tears and said, "When Amma gave me that name, it was like she had married me. And in giving it to someone else, it is like she has asked for a divorce!"

When Amma heard this, she couldn't help but laugh. She went on to explain to all the devotees around her that this girl was practicing Self-inquiry to understand the all-pervasive nature of the Self—to understand that the 'I' in me is the very same 'I' in all beings in the universe. Yet, when Amma named someone else "All-Pervasive," she became upset. Amma then asked, "Can there be two all-pervasives? Can there be two infinites?"

Of course not. It's impossible. This sincere devotee forgot the spiritual principle implied by her name—that all are one. Amma was lovingly pointing out that more assimilation of that truth was needed.

For full assimilation to take place, there can be no gap whatsoever between the knowledge of who we are and our thoughts, words, and actions. To see the complete assimilation of spiritual truth, all we have to do is look at Amma. Amma's thoughts, words, and deeds harmonize perfectly with the truths of *Vedanta*.

In Amritapuri, when I am trying to go from my room to see Amma on the darshan stage, which is a distance of about two hundred feet, it can take me as long as thirty minutes to get there. This is because so many devotees approach me with their questions and problems. If I start to feel impatient, I ask myself, "If my Atma and their Atma are one and the same, then their problems are my problems, their sorrows are my sorrows, their happiness is my happiness. So, why am I becoming impatient?"

In order to manifest this understanding in our thoughts, words, and actions, we must make it a priority. The very moment they arise we have to *see* our negativities and reflect. In this way, our negativities themselves can prod us to become more aware.

If we have trouble doing this, there is another method we can use: We can think about Amma. If, despite our Vedantic inquiry, we still feel our impatience growing, we can think of Amma's patience. Sometimes I think to myself, "Why are you getting impatient just because a few dozen people want to speak to you? Look how many people are lining up to see Amma to tell her their problems." If Amma were to walk two hundred feet and listen to the problems of everyone who approached her, it would not take her thirty minutes; it would take her thirty hours!

Please understand, I'm not comparing myself with Amma. What we do is truly infinitesimal compared to what Amma is doing. But when we reflect in this way, taking one of Amma's qualities as a touchstone, it helps us develop that same quality in ourselves. For example, if we reflect on Amma's patience, we will gradually develop more patience. And as long as we understand that the source of Amma's patience is her oneness with the Atma, we are doing more than developing a good quality. We are engaging in true Vedantic reflection.

Another very effective method to bridge the gap between our thoughts and actions is to keep a journal. Amma suggests this time and time again because it works. I know I mentioned journaling before, but I am repeating it here because this practice transforms lives.

Moving from the first stage of knowledge to the second stage of assimilation is a lifetime process. But Amma makes us all a promise: One day, every single one of us will attain the Atma jnanam degree. It is our birthright. It is just a matter of time. It cannot be otherwise because the Atma is our true nature. All we have to do is put in earnest effort. With Amma as our guide, we cannot go wrong. One day, just like Amma, we will all have doctorates in happiness.

24—The Power of Thanksgiving

On Thanksgiving Day in America, there is a tradition where everyone at the table shares what they are thankful for. People often say things like "friends and family," "health," or "prosperity." And, of course, they always express gratitude for the meal itself. This ritual has a way of awakening happiness and putting everyone in the holiday spirit. And yet, no matter how many words of gratitude we share, it can never be enough. We should learn to be thankful for everything, absolutely everything in creation.

Let me share what Amma said about gratitude as she was receiving a humanitarian award in Paris:

Shouldn't we give thanks to the chair we are sitting on right now? Shouldn't we express our gratitude to Mother Earth, who patiently provides her lap for us to run, jump and play on our whole life? Shouldn't we be grateful to the birds that sing for us, the flowers that blossom for us, the trees that give shade to us, and the rivers that flow for us? Each dawn, we are greeted with a new sunrise. At night, when we forget everything and sleep, anything could happen to us, even death. Do we ever thank the Great Power that blesses us to wake up the next morning and function normally as we face a new day? If we step back and look at the world this way, we will find that we have much more to be grateful for than we ever imagined. In fact, shouldn't we be grateful for absolutely everything? And above all, shouldn't we be grateful to God. Without God, there is nothing for us here, nothing at all – no earth to stand on, no space to move in, no air to breathe... nothing.

Amma tells a story that goes like this. It seems God was once approached by a scientist who said, "Listen, God, the scientific community had a high-level conference, and I regret to inform you that we decided we don't need you anymore. Now that we have learned how to clone people, transplant organs, and regenerate the body with stem cells, we don't really need you around."

"Oh, I see," God replied. "Well, if you would be so kind, would you join me in one final act of creation before I go? Let's each make a human being." The scientist agreed. God proposed they do it like he did in the good old days.

"Fine," replied the scientist, bending down to scoop up a handful of dirt.

"Wait!" said God, shaking his head in disapproval. "Not so fast."

"What's wrong?" asked the scientist.

"Well," God replied, "You have to make your own dirt."

We take so much for granted in life. Amma, however, says that everything should be seen and accepted with thanks. Amma embodies this kind of gratitude. She bows down to everything, even the safety pins that fasten her sari. Her every action expresses gratitude to the Supreme Being.

Once, after having given darshan all night at a program far away from the ashram, Amma travelled all day to return to Amritapuri. She returned late in the evening. As she stepped into her room, Amma said, "I am so sorry I missed the evening bhajans." Her voice carried a tone of regret.

"To sing the Lord's name is such a precious gift," she said. "It is a chance to express our love and gratitude for all that he gives us." In that quiet moment, those present were deeply touched not just by her words, but by the sincerity and longing behind them. "I didn't sing God's divine names today," she sighed. "So, I don't deserve to eat anything." And that is exactly what she did. She didn't eat until after bhajans finished the following day.

Just imagine what would happen to us if we held ourselves to the same standard. We would all surely starve to death!

In the Indian tradition, the attitude of thankfulness that inspires personal sacrifice is known as *yajna*. In yajna, I acknowledge that everything in this world, from the earth that I stand upon to the air I breathe, from the food I eat to the sun that gives me light—all of this is freely given by God. And this realization inspires me to gratefully sacrifice for others.

In our lives, if we so much as borrow a pen from someone, we say, "Thank you." So, shouldn't we be saying a huge thanks to God for everything we are receiving? Thanksgiving is a day when we remember to say thank you to the Lord. Yajna is when we keep that spirit alive *throughout our life*, every day, in every action.

There is a touching story I once heard about Thanksgiving. The day before Thanksgiving vacation, a first-grade teacher asked each of her students to draw something that they were grateful for. Most of the children drew pictures of turkeys or of their families. But one student with learning disabilities drew a picture of a hand.

Because of his condition, most of the other children did not play with him very much. He often spent recess alone on the swing set. Sometimes he just stood near the teacher. But for once, he had the full attention of the class. A hand? Why had he drawn a hand? The class was captivated.

"I think it must be the hand of God that brings us food," one student said.

"No, it's a farmer's hand," said another, "because they grow the turkeys."

"More like a policeman, because they protect us," quipped another.

"I think it is supposed to be all the hands that help us," chimed in yet another student.

"But he only drew one of them," the student next to him muttered.

Finally, the teacher asked the little boy, "So, whose hand is this?"

The little boy mumbled, "It's yours."

At that moment, the teacher recalled that from time to time she had taken the little boy by the hand; she often did that with children. But it meant so much to this little boy that it changed his life, and he eventually overcame his learning disabilities. Gratitude for everything — the big, the small, and all the God-given things we often take for granted — is something we can all try to integrate into our lives.

Listen now to a different kind of story that highlights the lack of gratitude that is all too common these days. After a man died, he reached heaven and was welcomed by an angel. The angel said, "Since you're new here, I will take you on a brief tour."

After visiting many dazzling places in heaven, they reached a spot with a couple of high-rise buildings. The first one was almost as tall as the Regency Hotel in New York. The angel showed the man a few rooms, each of which contained stacks of letters piled all the way to the ceiling.

"What are all these letters?" asked the newcomer curiously.

"They are prayer requests and demands from people on Earth. All of these have been answered by the Lord."

"Oh, my gosh!" the man said. "Human beings make this many demands on God?"

"Yes, indeed," replied the angel.

Next, they entered the other high-rise building, which also had lots and lots of rooms on every floor, just like the first building. The difference was that these rooms had hardly any papers in them at all.

"Are these also requests?" asked the man.

"No, they are thank-you letters to God for fulfilled prayers. We only get a handful of them every year."

But Amma's children are not like this. They strive to show their gratitude by living lives in harmony with Amma's teachings. Amma says, we need not give big things. Often, the small things we give, like a heartfelt smile, a kind word, a compassionate ear, can be even bigger than the so-called big things.

To be honest, it would take forever to express our gratitude to creation the way we should. Just imagine trying to thank each of the microorganisms in our stomach for helping us digest our food. It would be impossible. But we need not do that. Because Amma is an enlightened being who is one with creation, whatever we offer to her benefits everything and everyone. So, instead of trying to thank each and every creature, we can serve Amma. By doing this, we are repaying our debts to all beings everywhere. At the same time, we can offer whatever we do for others as an expression of gratitude to God.

The final thing I would like to point out is that Thanksgiving is always celebrated on a Thursday. In Indian tradition, Thursday is the day dedicated to the guru. The person who deserves the most appreciation of all is the guru, for the guru can make up for our shortcomings, absorb our prarabdha karma, and give us liberation, taking us beyond all bondage. Amma truly deserves infinite thanks from each of us. What an immense blessing that we are all with Amma, a living manifestation of God. Because we can see, touch, and talk to her, Amma's form solidifies our relationship with the universal energy and the consciousness flowing through all of creation.

25—Let Her Sacrifice Change You

Nothing Amma does is for herself. Her every thought, word, and deed is for others. In the *Bhagavad Gita*, Sri Krishna comments on such selflessness—*loka-saṅgraham evāpi sampaśhyan kartum arhasi*: "The enlightened one acts only with an eye to uplift the world" (3.20). When we reflect on Amma's actions, it is important to remember this: Amma has nothing to gain. Her very Self *is* the source of all bliss and contentment. She knows that she can never lose this. And so, whether she is giving satsang, singing bhajans, managing the ashram's charitable programs, or sitting with us in meditation, Amma has nothing to gain. She does these things for our sake, to set an example for us to follow.

As Amma's devotees, it is essential that we grasp this. If we want our bond with Amma to deepen, we have to understand the profound sacrifice Amma is making for our upliftment. As Amma so often says, "The guru verily *lives* for the disciple." If Amma wanted to, she could simply lie in bed all day. There are many people who would be more than willing to take care of her. There is no need whatsoever for Amma to lead a disciplined life. But for our sake, Amma leads the most disciplined life possible, hoping that we will imitate her and become disciplined as well.

We can see a visible sign of Amma's discipline and sacrifice every night at the end of the program when devotees offer *arati* to Amma. Before the corona pandemic, this only happened when Amma toured abroad. It wasn't possible in Amritapuri because Amma almost always left the hall right after bhajans, before arati started.

This created a problem, though. Towards the end of bhajans, as Amma got up to leave, about three hundred ashramites would jump to their feet and stampede towards Amma's house. They all wanted to get a good spot, so they could see her walk up the stairs to her room. Seeing this time and again, Amma finally scolded the ashramites, explaining to them that arati was an important part of the bhajans. Without it, the bhajan-worship was incomplete. But there was another problem. The three hundred stampeding ashramites often trampled on those who *did* stay for the arati.

Amma scolded them once, twice, three times ... so many times. Almost no one listened. This left Amma with only one choice: She started staying for the arati. Even though she had much work to do, even though she had not eaten all day, even though she felt some people might get the wrong idea seeing her worshiped in this way, she started staying for arati. This meant that Amma would have less time in the evenings to have meetings, make phone calls, and read letters. This is the depth of the self-sacrifice that Amma constantly makes for us.

In fact, Amma says, "It is only because of the guru's sacrifice and patience that the disciple reaches the goal." If we want to grow spiritually, it is essential that we imbibe Amma's self-sacrifice. We need to learn to sacrifice for the good of others too. We cannot continue to miss this message. I'm not saying we are lazy, but we can all definitely put Amma's teachings into practice more fully if we really try.

It's not that we have to stay up late with Amma or eat only a handful of food every day like she does. We should understand our limitations and then do what we can to integrate Amma's teachings into our lives. With this thought in mind, let's revisit the *Gita* verse from the beginning of this chapter: "The enlightened one acts only with an eye to uplift the world." Our Satguru Amma is the perfect embodiment of those words. She lives solely to help others. Through her example she is modeling love and sacrifice for us. If we her children fail to integrate these qualities, all of Amma's sacrifice and all of the physical pain she endures on our behalf will be in vain.

To better understand Amma's sacrifice, just try this on one of her international tours. Clear your calendar for one day, come to the program, and do everything Amma does. I don't mean you should give darshan, but come to the hall when Amma does, and then just watch Amma give darshan. You can sit near Amma for some time, then you can go sit on a chair in the main hall and watch Amma on one of the TV screens. You can move from place to place if you want but keep watching Amma. Watch her throughout the darshan. When she leaves, you can go eat something light and then rest. (As for Amma, she doesn't rest much during break times. Instead, she starts going through the hundreds of letters that have arrived for her that day. But we will make a concession for ourselves.)

Then when Amma returns to the hall for the evening program, do the same. Be there for her arrival, meditate with Amma, listen to the satsang, sing the bhajans, perform the arati, and then just watch again. Watch Amma with one-pointed concentration. Stay with Amma. Just keep going for as long as she gives darshan, even if she finishes at 3:30 in the morning. After that, even though Amma stays up working and reading letters until sunrise, you can go to sleep.

We can only understand the strain of carrying a heavy weight after we ourselves have tried to do so. This is why we should all spend at least one day following Amma's schedule. It is a small way we can begin to fathom the self-sacrifice she endures for our upliftment. Nothing can better strengthen our bond with Amma. Nothing can help us better understand the depth of her love for us. Nothing can better inspire us to embody the principles she works so hard to teach us day in and day out. After your day with Amma, take time to contemplate the wonder that she has served this way without rest for more than five decades.

When Amma's father, Sugunanandan Acchan, passed away, Amma was in Kolkata, the final city of her North India Tour. As soon as the program was over, we all traveled back to Kerala for the cremation.

Before the funeral, Amma sat in vigil next to her father's body for three days. Now, to be honest, Amma sees everyone in the universe as her relative. Even that is an understatement. Amma sees everyone in the universe as her very own Self. Even so, Amma was Acchan's daughter, and she had a dharma to fulfill towards him and the family.

But why did Amma sit by her father's body for three days? It would have been more than enough for her to come to the final prayers and cremation. But because Acchan was Amma's father, thousands of people wanted to come and pay their respects—devotees, villagers, politicians, and government officials. In the end, Amma knew that the only way the swamis and ashramites would properly host the guests was if she made their presence known. By sitting with her father's body, she made the steady flow of visitors impossible to miss.

Amma had just finished an eight-week tour of India, driving along the bumpy roads and giving darshan in dusty venues to an estimated 400,000 people. Physically, she was not well. But to ensure that we would do our dharma and serve the guests, she maintained the vigil. When Amma told me this, it hit me square in the heart. After thirty years as her disciple, Amma continues to sacrifice herself for my benefit, for all of our benefit, that we may gain the discipline and maturity required to reach the final goal of spiritual life.

We may be rusty iron, but Amma sees the potential, the latent power hidden within each of us. This is why Amma consistently calls us beyond ourselves, inviting us to embody the same sacrifice and love she so effortlessly gives. This spirit of sacrifice is the essence of selfless service, the light that guides us forward.

Part 3: Love and Service

26—The Power of Pure Love

From the spirit of selfless sacrifice springs the greatest transformative force in our spiritual journey: Amma's love. For decades, devotees have pondered the mystery of this love, which is why so many books in the Amma Shop are devoted to this theme. This might lead you to think Amma's love is something complex, but in truth, it may be the simplest thing in the universe. Ironically, it's often that very simplicity that causes us to overlook its depth.

To experience Amma's love, we need only spend some time with Amma. But if we want to cultivate that love in ourselves, we have to dive deep. Only then will we see love's full glory and understand the endless patience and compassion underlying it.

Before we explore divine love, let's think about worldly love because it's the kind most people are familiar with. Let me share a brief story from the great epic *Mahabharata* to begin our exploration.

At one point in the story, the hero, Arjuna, travels to heaven to help the king of the gods fight against a horde of demons. After the battle, Arjuna celebrates victory with the gods. As part of the celebration, a heavenly damsel named Urvashi dances for the king and his guests.

As she dances, she sees Arjuna at the king's side and is smitten. Overcome by his strength and good looks, she decides she wants him for herself. After the dance, she quickly puts on her fanciest dress, sprays on perfume, and combs her hair. Only then does she go to Arjuna's room to profess her love.

But there is a problem: Arjuna is not interested.

The English poet William Congreve once wrote, "Hell hath no fury like a woman scorned." Urvashi proves Congreve knew what he was talking about. From Urvashi's perspective, Arjuna's behavior was outrageous. After all, she was a heavenly being professing love for a mere mortal. His rejection was insane, so she cursed him, saying, "Since you are acting like a eunuch, may you become a eunuch!" As you may know, in such legends, curses always come true. Although Urvashi lived in heaven, her love for Arjuna was worldly, not divine. It was not true love. True love is pure and selfless. It is never angry.

Later in the epic, Krishna teaches Arjuna that selfish desire is the root of all anger. Anger is always the result of thwarted desire. So, if we ever find our love turning into anger, it is proof that our love still has some degree of selfishness mixed into it. Angry love is not pure love.

Amma says pure, selfless love is the one thing the entire world is seeking. Unfortunately, it is the one thing most people are not receiving. This is why so many are overwhelmed when they first meet Amma. She is the first person in their lives who has ever given them pure, selfless love. Before we met Amma, it was as if we were trying to quench our thirst with stagnant water. But in Amma's arms, we finally receive our first drink of cool, pure water.

A devotee explained her experience of Amma's embrace like this: "When I was young my parents didn't want me to eat chocolate. So, they gave me carob, a chocolate substitute, and told me that it was chocolate. For years I went on eating carob, thinking it was the real thing. One day a friend gave me real chocolate. As soon as I bit into it, I knew I would never be satisfied with carob again."

This is how it is for many people when they first receive Amma's darshan. For the first time in their lives, they encounter the real thing, pure love.

What many people don't understand, though, is that the love, the peace, the bliss that they experience in Amma's arms is not something external. The love is coming from within them. In Amma's arms, they experience their own true nature. As a breeze temporarily clears away the fog covering a lake, Amma's gentle, loving embrace clears the negativity and desires from the mind. What shines forth in that moment is the bliss of our True Self.

This is the mystery of Amma's darshan. Somehow it awakens the immense bliss and love inside us and transforms our lives. Gradually we stop seeking material happiness in the outer world and begin seeking spiritual happiness in the inner world.

Let me tell you a true story. Once a young man wanted a raise, but his boss rejected his request. This made the young man very angry, but he was clever. Seeing Amma's photo on his boss's desk, he realized that Amma was his boss's Big Boss. So, the young man went straight to Amma's ashram to plead his case. Amma listened intently and finally said, "Okay, you tell your boss that you spoke to Amma and that she says he should help you." Amma also assured the young man she would say this directly to the boss the next time he came for darshan.

The next morning, the young man headed straight to his boss's office and said, "Amma says you owe me a raise."

The boss retorted, "I will talk to Amma about this myself."

But the boss did not go to see Amma that week, or the week after. Soon a full month passed, then two. There was no sign of a raise. Fed up, the young man decided to go to Amritapuri to give Amma an update. While waiting in the darshan line, he prepared his argument. He was ready to expose his boss's lack of devotion and complete disregard for Amma's instructions.

As the line inched forward, Amma kept looking at him. Every time he looked up at Amma, Amma was looking back with a mischievous smile. His anger toward his boss began to dissolve, and in its place, a deep love for Amma began to awaken. When he finally fell into Amma's arms, all he could say was, "Amma, I don't want to work for him anymore. I want to stay here and work selflessly for you." He resigned from his job and now lives in the ashram working tirelessly for Amma's charitable mission. This is how it is with pure love: it shifts our focus from the material back to the spiritual.

27—Compassion Flows From Self-Knowledge

Once a sick girl came for Amma's darshan. She had just thrown up, which I could tell because she still had vomit on her shirt. As she approached Amma, the smell spread everywhere. One of the people helping with the darshan line turned around, saw the state of the girl, and immediately pushed her away saying, "Hey—go, go, go, go, go! Go clean yourself up."

Amma saw the volunteer's reaction and said, "Let the girl come."

Full of compassion, Amma pulled the sick girl forward, took out her own hand towel, and began gently wiping the vomit off the girl. She spent several minutes cleaning her up. When Amma was finished, she took the girl into her arms for a heartfelt embrace.

For me, this was a beautiful illustration of the difference between someone who has fully assimilated Self-knowledge and someone who has not. At the heart of true Self-knowledge lies boundless compassion, free from judgment and filled with an immediate, natural impulse to help.

At the time, I noticed my own reaction. It was also one of aversion. But Amma's spontaneous reaction was completely different. It was one of love and compassion. Afterwards, Amma turned to the volunteer and asked, "If that had been your daughter, would you have chased her away like that?"

Let's all start emulating Amma's example in our lives, beginning with the simple things she does that touch us so deeply. We don't have to be a Realized Soul to smile peacefully at others or to listen patiently when they open their hearts to us. Even without a firm foundation in the scriptures, we can mirror Amma's example of humility in our interactions with others. Though we may not be adept spiritual practitioners, we can still try to love our family members without expectation, just as Amma loves us.

28—Always Give More

True compassion expresses itself in action. It calls us to devote time and energy to serving others, even when we feel stretched to the limit. Amma's life teaches us that even in our busiest moments, there is still space to give, as the story below illustrates.

One day a teacher stood before his class with several items arranged on the table in front of him. He picked up a large, empty jar and started filling it with pebbles. When the pebbles reached the top of the jar, he asked his students, "Is the jar full?"

"Yes!" they responded in chorus.

He then took a canister of sand and poured it into the jar. Gradually, the sand filtered down, filling in the spaces between the pebbles. The teacher asked the students again, "Is it full now?"

"Yes!" the students replied.

But the teacher wasn't done yet. He took a flask of water from the table and poured all of it into the jar—every last drop fit. The teacher explained, "This experiment is here to teach you something important. Many feel like their lives are so busy that there's no time left for anything else. But if we pause and reflect, we'll see we actually have more time than we realize. To live well, we need to make the very best use of the time we've been given."

Like the students in the story, we often feel that we have no time. But when we look at Amma's life, we see that, even though she has so much to do, she always finds time and often new ways to serve, no matter what the circumstances.

Before the Covid pandemic, Amma used to spend the two weeks right before the annual U.S. Summer Tour to give private darshan to all the ashram residents. For many of the ashramites, this time alone with Amma was their only opportunity to ask her questions about their lives, their spiritual practices, and their seva. During this time, Amma could not give public darshan.

Instead, she dutifully stayed in her room for two straight weeks counseling ashramite after ashramite, one after the other.

But one year, something unusual happened. Many more visitors than usual descended on Amritapuri. Many of them had never met Amma before. When they went to the office to ask if they could meet Amma, they were told, "Sorry, it's just not possible this time of year."

When Amma heard about this, she decided to create more space in her already packed schedule like the teacher in the story. She called the office and said, "Start sending the newcomers to my room in groups of twenty. They can sit in the back while room darshans are going on."

The solution was a total win-win. The ashram residents got to ask Amma their personal questions, and everyone else got to spend time with Amma and receive her prasad. The volunteers in the office thought the jar was full, but Amma knew a secret they didn't: There is almost always more space in the jar.

This is how it has always been with Amma. Her life has always been full to the brim, but each year she somehow manages to do more—to see more people, to travel to more places, and to give more of herself in increasingly creative ways. Recently, Amma created yet another priceless opportunity for all who visit Amritapuri: the chance to perform *arati* to her individually at the end of bhajans.

This reminds me of a story about how challenging it can be to manage different responsibilities at the same time. Once, a businessman from New England went to Orlando to resolve some issues with clients. To make his wife happy, he decided to turn the trip into a vacation and bought her tickets to join him after his meetings.

Amidst the negotiations, the husband secretly tried to send his wife an email but accidentally mistyped her address. At that very moment, somewhere in Houston, a widow, who was riding back from her husband's funeral, received this shocking email:

Honey,
Surprise! It's me! I managed to get online. I checked in a few hours ago. Don't worry. Everything has been prepared for your arrival tomorrow. Looking forward to seeing you then! Hope your journey will be as smooth as mine was.
P.S. It sure is hot down here!

Like this businessman, most of us find multitasking a challenge, but it's not an issue for Amma. She puts even the most high-powered multi-taskers to shame. If you're not sure about this, just watch Amma give darshan. While her main goal is to embrace people and give them her focused attention, she is doing so much more. As people rest in her arms, she is often discussing the ashram's humanitarian activities at the same time. It's a win-win because the devotees in her arms often receive longer-than-normal darshans while these conversations are taking place.

But Amma is doing much more than this. She is answering questions about spiritual practices and personal matters... giving spiritual names... looking at devotees across the room... troubleshooting to make sure everyone has a comfortable place to sit... throwing chocolates at those who have fallen asleep... and critiquing the mixing of the sound system. This list doesn't even begin to scratch the surface. Just the other day while Amma was hugging, she was simultaneously singing an old Tamil film song that a devotee wanted to hear her sing.

Amazingly, all of these examples are only on the gross level. Who knows what all Amma is doing on the subtle level? Only by watching Amma can we truly begin to grasp why Hindu goddesses are often depicted with as many as six, eight, or even eighteen hands!

29—In Giving We Receive

The Padmabhushan is a prestigious award given by the Government of India to individuals who have demonstrated excellence in their field of work. It is a great honor. But it is not as great an honor as the Padmavibhushan, and the Padmavibhushan is not as great an honor as the Government's highest award, the Bharat Ratna.

A few years ago, when the annual bestowal of these awards was taking place, the Padmabhushan was given as a lifetime achievement award to a famous classical vocalist. But when offered the award, she refused to accept it, saying, "The Government should have recognized my singing long before this. And besides, you have given many lesser singers than I the Padmavibhushan, while only offering me the Padmabhushan. I don't want your award."

Now, let me tell you a contrasting story about one of Amma's devotees. Despite her impressive education, this devotee had a very difficult government job that did not pay very much. And, believe me, no one was rushing forward to give her a Padmabhushan, Padmavibhushan, or Bharat Ratna. Nevertheless, she knew that the work she was doing was helping to reduce medical expenses for poor people. And this, she told Amma, was more than enough reward for her. She was happy, content, and lived with a sense of fullness. Unlike the vocalist, Amma's daughter was more focused on what she could do for others than what others could do for her.

Amma says this is how our lives should be. If you want contentment, if you want satisfaction, if you want that sense of fullness and completeness, then don't focus on what you can take, focus on what you can give. If you focus only on taking, you will always see what you are missing. If you focus on giving, you will always see what you have. What's more, you may not always be in a position to receive. But no matter who you are, no matter where you are, you are always in a position to give.

Amma is the ultimate giver. She never looks at what she can take, but only at what she can give. I recall a beautiful example from 2006, when Amma received the James Parks Morton Interfaith Award in New York. When we heard the organization had chosen Amma as their winner, I wanted to know what they were going to do for Amma. What would the award be? A trophy? A check? A first-class trip to Tahiti for Amma and her disciples? Out of curiosity, I kept pestering Amma for more information. Finally, Amma said, "Look. I am not going to New York to *get* something. I'm going there to see what I can give. So, stop bothering me."

It was yet another situation where Amma was pointing out to me that I was focused on the wrong thing. I was trying to see what could be taken, while Amma was thinking about what we could give. Unlike me, Amma was preparing to share wisdom during her address at the awards ceremony and brainstorming practical ways to support the organization that was hosting her.

How beautiful it would have been if that classical singer had a slightly more expansive perspective. She could have taken so much joy in knowing that millions of people enjoyed her singing. She could have thanked God for having blessed her with her talent. As Krishna says in the *Gita*, "Wherever you see greatness, you should understand that it is not the greatness of the individual but the greatness of God that is manifesting" (10.40). But, no, this singer was only focused on herself.

Giving is not a small thing. Amma says, "If we are able to give just one person one minute of happiness, we should consider it as a great blessing."

Amma says that God has given each and every one of us special talents, and it is up to us to discover and develop them. But the point of doing so is not to become great in the eyes of others. Talents are not meant to help us gain name, fame, or personal glory; they are given so we can help, uplift, and inspire others, like Amma does.

Let me share an example from Amma's life. In the early 1980s, when the ashram had only a few thatched huts and just six or seven disciples, we were all living hand to mouth. It was a beautiful time, but it was not easy. It was austere back then, but we never felt the harshness of it because we were all so immersed in Amma's love and compassion. Only when I look back now do I realize how simply we were living. We only had enough money to eat one full meal a day. And the other swamis and I had only a few decent shirts amongst us, which we would share according to the need of the day.

One day a devotee who was an expert in vastu came to the ashram. Remember, earlier I explained that vastu is the ancient Indian science of architecture. Anyway, seeing the layout of the ashram, this devotee immediately told me that it was inauspicious. He pointed to a large ungated area through which many people entered the ashram and said, "You cannot leave that open. If you leave it open like that, all your wealth will exit through there." I took him very seriously and immediately brought him up to tell Amma.

Amma listened to him and said in reply, "Son, I want it like that. For you, such a layout may be inauspicious because from your perspective, losing wealth is a negative thing. But from my point of view, this is the most auspicious thing possible. I am not interested in taking and accumulating. I am only interested in giving. We have not built this ashram for our gain. We have built this ashram for the upliftment of the world. We are here to help the poor, the needy, and the suffering. We are not here to take."

It's hard to have an expansive vision like Amma's when we have all been conditioned to think in the exact opposite way. This reminds me of a story... Once a man who was raising donations for a charity decided to call the town's most successful lawyer. When he finally got the lawyer on the phone, he said, "Sir, you are so successful, and you make so much money. Wouldn't you like to give back to the community in some way?"

The lawyer was silent for a moment, then replied: "Are you aware that my mother is dying after a long illness and has medical bills that are several times her annual income?"

Embarrassed, the man mumbled, "Uh... no."

"Or that my brother, a disabled veteran, is blind and confined to a wheelchair?"

The embarrassed volunteer began to stammer out an apology, but the lawyer interrupted, saying, "Or that my sister's husband died in a traffic accident, leaving her penniless with three children?!"

The humiliated charity worker, completely beaten down, quietly mumbled, "I had no idea..."

The lawyer cut him off yet again, his voice rising with indignation, and said, "So, if I didn't give any money to them, then why would I give any money to you?"

Why do so many people find it difficult to be open-hearted and generous? I'm not talking about money. I'm talking about sharing time, kindness, patience, knowledge, or even just a smile. Amma says that when we choose not to give it's because we believe we are our limited body and mind. When we think we are limited, we think of giving as losing, and that makes us feel insecure.

Amma knows she is not limited, and so her entire life has become a celebration of giving and sharing. She knows that no matter how much she gives, it can never affect her real Self. Whether we are rich or poor, educated or ignorant, heavy or thin... No external condition can ever change the fullness of our true Self.

I would like to conclude with an extraordinary story of giving... Ten years ago, when Amma was touring in northern Kerala, an extremely large crowd came for Amma's 7 p.m. program. The darshan went on throughout the night. At 9:00 a.m. the next morning Amma was still giving darshan. Late in the program, a devotee asked Amma if she would stop by his house before she drove on to Bangalore. Amma agreed. By this point, Amma had been sitting on the stage for fourteen hours without any food or rest. I couldn't believe his audacity. The next day would bring another large darshan, and here was this man pestering Amma to come to his house! Despite the late hour, Amma assured him that she would come.

When darshan finally finished, we learned that the man's house was completely out of the way. After half an hour or so, we arrived. Amma gracefully alighted from her camper, looking as fresh as ever, and entered the man's house. She did a simple *puja* in the prayer room after which the man asked Amma to visit yet another room. I couldn't believe my ears! It seemed it wasn't enough that Amma had come to his house. This man wanted Amma to enter and bless each and every room. But, yet again, Amma gracefully agreed.

When we entered the next room, I suddenly realized why Amma had agreed to come to this house. There on the bed was a child. His legs and arms were shrunk like toothpicks, and his head was more than double the size of a normal head. His head was so large that he could not lift it without assistance. There was no way he could have come to the program. Amma held the child, cradled his head in her arms, and fed him prasad with her own hands, while lovingly repeating, "My son, my son, my son" in his ear. I felt so ashamed of my anger towards the boy's father and admonished myself for second-guessing Amma.

Amma was exhausted. The darshan had continued well past sunrise, and darshan the following day would likely be just as long. Such physical strain is not good for Amma's health, and she is surely aware of this. But because she is one with the True Self, Amma chose to ignore her body. Only one thing mattered to her: One of her children was alone and in pain, and she had the power to bring him comfort.

Amma is the pinnacle of giving. Only where there is unfathomable love and unfathomable spiritual knowledge can selflessness express itself in this way. With Amma's grace, may all of us gradually acquire such expansive vision, and thereby become lights in the darkness.

30—The Guru Reveals Our Divinity

In today's world, it seems everyone is a guru or a teacher. We have fashion gurus, technology gurus, investment gurus, sports gurus, gossip gurus. The following verse from the *Guru Gita* cuts through the fog and defines what a real Guru is:

gukārastvandhakāro vai rukārastannirvartakaḥ |
andhakāra nivartivāt guru vityabhidhīyate || (17)

The syllable *gu* is darkness, and the syllable *ru* stands for its eliminator. He is called Guru because he removes the darkness.

Darkness symbolizes ignorance. And so, the fashion guru removes ignorance about fashion. The technology guru sheds light on technology, and the gossip guru shines a spotlight on everyone's dirty laundry.

What type of Guru is Amma? In Sanskrit, we say she is a Satguru. *Sat* means "pure truth, pure existence, pure reality, pure being." So, just as the technology guru sheds light on technology, Amma sheds light on the ultimate Truth.

How blessed we are to have Amma to help us understand and assimilate this ultimate reality. If Amma were a chemistry guru, most of us wouldn't be interested. In fact, if we think back to the periodic table, and our high school teacher scolding us for not knowing the atomic number of hydrogen, we'd probably run the other way. On some level, we have come to Amma because we sense that spiritual knowledge is liberating. We believe it is knowledge that will give us peace, bliss, and a sense of security, and we believe Amma can give us this knowledge.

But in this day and age, many people think that a guru is just a boss, someone who has tricked everyone into serving them and obeying them while they sit back and enjoy themselves.

This is probably because we have read about so-called gurus who acted like this. But it is not like this with Amma. She leads us, but she also works harder than any of us.

Once, a man went to a pet store to buy an exotic bird. The old shopkeeper showed him three identical parrots and said, "The one on the left costs $500, and the one in the middle costs $1,000."

The man pointed to the left and asked, "Why does that one cost $500?"

The shopkeeper replied, "Because he knows how to use a computer."

"What about the one in the middle?" the man asked. "Why is he double the price?"

The old shopkeeper answered, "Because he can do everything the first parrot can do, and he knows Excel."

Intrigued, the man asked, "Well, what about the third parrot?"

"He costs $2,000," the old man replied.

"Well, what can he do?" asked the man.

"To be honest," said the shopkeeper, "I've never seen him do a thing, but the other two parrots call him boss."

Amma is not like this third parrot at all. She does everything we do and a thousand times more. And that is only on the gross level. Who knows what Amma is doing on the subtle level!

Of course, we know Amma gives darshan. But have we ever thought about who provides the music for the programs? Well, it's Amma. Who leads meditation? Amma. Who leads the world peace prayer? Amma. Who serves the food on all the retreats and tour-group stops? Amma. In India, Amma even organizes transportation for poor devotees, makes announcements about possible thieves in the crowd, and serves prasad meals to the ashramites. If you look at any job in the ashram, at some point or other over the years, Amma herself has done it.

Once a journalist asked Amma, "Amma, were you ever interested in family life and children?"

Amma's response was beautiful. "Daughter," she said, "everything in creation is my child."

Later in the interview, she fine-tuned this idea slightly, saying, "Actually, when it comes to my spiritual children, I'm only a midwife, who helps them give birth to the divinity within."

This attitude is typical of real mahatmas like Amma. In fact, long ago, another mahatma, the Greek philosopher Socrates, directly compared himself to a midwife as well. This isn't surprising, since his mother had been a midwife. Once, while reflecting on his role as a guru, Socrates said: "My art of midwifery is just like a regular midwife's in most respects. The difference is that I watch over the labor of souls, not of bodies."

Socrates was speaking on two levels here: the *paravidya* and *aparavidya* levels. Paravidya is supreme Self-knowledge, the knowledge that liberates us, and aparavidya is worldly knowledge. Socrates' vision was expansive, and so it came naturally to him to share both worldly and supreme knowledge with his disciples.

Just like Socrates, Amma is sharing both kinds of knowledge with humanity. She is imparting spiritual knowledge to help us discover the divinity within. At the same time, Amma is helping us acquire practical knowledge, so we can serve the poor, the sick, the needy, and society at large.

Let me share an example of this that took place at Amma's top-ranked university in India. From the start, Amma has insisted that all research-and-development projects at Amrita University focus on uplifting those who struggle. Inspired by this noble goal, the university has created and deployed wireless landslide detectors to protect hillside villagers from catastrophe. It has developed low-cost glucose strips to help diabetes patients monitor their sugar levels. It has even created a free app to help people become literate in English. That project won an award from the Barbara Bush Foundation in the United States. To be honest, there are far too many life-changing Amrita projects to list here.

Every time an Amrita University department wins an award, the department heads always say that they owe all their success to Amma. They say this without fail, every single time. It gets to the point that you start to wonder if it's just lip-service. But when you speak with these department heads, they share the most amazing stories—stories revealing that Amma was the midwife to every one of these ideas.

Not long ago, Amma was speaking with the director of the Amrita School of Biotechnology. He told Amma that he wanted to help diabetes patients, who often take a long time to heal from cuts and bruises. Amma casually mentioned that in her village they used to treat wounds with the heated oil of cashew shells. At first, the idea of extracting medicine from something that is usually just thrown away seemed a bit odd, but he decided to investigate.

His team found that cashew nut shells contain anacardic acid. In the end, they scientifically demonstrated the effects of this acid and its potential healing properties. It seems this acid might even benefit people with certain kinds of cancer. Amrita continues with this research, which could hold tremendous benefits for humankind. Here, we clearly see Amma helping people gain practical knowledge to better serve the world.

As for knowledge of the ultimate truth, she guides us skillfully, unfolding our lessons patiently, step by step, creating the perfect circumstances to deliver us from our negativities and selfishness.

Please allow me to share an example from my own life. In the beginning of Amma's ashram, we all lived in huts made of thatched leaves. The tricky thing about huts is that there is no real privacy. If you are speaking inside the hut, people outside can hear you. And if you are speaking outside the hut, people inside can hear you.

One morning as I was trying to meditate in my hut, I heard two boys talking outside. They didn't know that I could hear them. I'd say they were thirteen or fourteen years old. It was early in the morning, and Amma was trying to get a little rest. She hadn't slept at all the night before.

One of the brahmacharis had just rushed over and told them to be quiet. The two boys were now complaining about this near my hut. Well, really it was mostly just one boy. The other one was listening. At one point, the boy who was doing all the talking said, "Who does that guy think he is to tell us to be quiet?" He followed up by calling the brahmachari a couple of choice bad words. I could hardly believe my ears.

Finally, he said, "Anyway, this ashram is nothing but a few dingy huts near stinking backwaters. I can't wait to get out of here. These guys are losers. Who do they think they are kidding? They are not real brahmacharis!" He then started boasting about the real swamis his father was friends with at a traditional ashram in a neighboring state.

Now, the thing is, I didn't even have to see the boy to know exactly who he was. His father was a rich businessman. Although I remained cool on the outside, on the inside I was fuming. What I really wanted to do was to grab him by the ear and throw him into our "stinking backwaters." But I knew that Amma would not like that, so I didn't say anything. My only consolation was that he and his father would be leaving in a few hours.

About two hours later Amma called me over and said, "Hey, the businessman who came here with his son is going to Kochi for the night. He wants to leave his son here until he gets back. I think he should stay with you."

I was dumbfounded. I wanted to give this kid a tight slap, not share my room with him! Why couldn't Amma let him stay with someone else? But Amma herself had said he was to stay with me, which meant it was my duty to treat him properly, like a guest. What else could I do?

So, I cleaned up my hut, cleared space for his sleeping mat, and invited him in.

Lucky for me, the first day I did not see much of him because I was running a lot of errands. But that night, something happened. Our young friend received a guest of his own, the doo-doo bug. He was up all night with diarrhea. I have a confession to make. My first thoughts were not compassionate. They were more along the lines of, "Thank you, Amma!"

But, of course, in huts there are no bathrooms or toilets. You have to go outside. And this fourteen-year-old boy had no experience of such things. On top of this, he was afraid of the dark. So, when he had to go to the toilet, I had to go with him, every time, all night long. In fact, I'm pretty sure I was suffering more than he was. But as we walked through the dark again and again something began to change in me. I gradually stopped seeing him as an arrogant, uncultured brat and saw him for what he really was, my little brother. My heart, which had hardened so much towards him, softened and opened up.

By the next day, he was doing better, and I began bringing him food and special water. We talked about his life, and he even began asking me about Amma and the spiritual path. By the time he left, both he and I had changed. My attitude towards him and his attitude towards Amma and her brahmacharis had completely flipped. Amma's midwifery was at work yet again! She foresaw the potential for change in both of us and created the perfect situation to bring it about.

Looping back to Socrates, he once said that, with God's grace all who associated with him would make progress. Some would even become brilliant. But he refused to take credit for any of their attainments, creative ideas, discoveries, or spiritual progress. When asked, he humbly said, "They simply discovered some of the many beautiful things that are within them."

And while Socrates took no credit for the beautiful creations of his disciples, he did take credit for their delivery. That was his role, to help his disciples manifest what was hidden within them. But what Socrates did was so subtle that many overlooked the value of his role in the process. They started asking, "Hey, what did this guy really do for us anyway?" As the following story demonstrates, it can be hard to appreciate subtlety...

Once, a giant ship engine failed. The ship's owners hired one expert after another, but none of them could figure out how to fix it. Finally, they brought in an old man who had been fixing ships since he was young. He carried a large bag of tools with him wherever he went.

When he arrived on the scene, he immediately went to work and carefully inspected the engine from top to bottom. Two of the ship's owners looked on anxiously, hoping he would know what to do. At last, he took out a small hammer and gently tapped a small screw. Instantly, the boat lurched to life. The engine was fixed.

A week later, the owners received a bill for $10,000.

"What?" the owners exclaimed. "He hardly did anything!"

They hastily wrote the old man a terse note: "Please send us an itemized bill." The old man replied in an equally terse way, "Tapping with hammer, $2.00. Knowing where to tap, $9,998."

It is the same with the guru. What Amma does is often so subtle that we fail to appreciate its value. It is up to us to ensure we do not forget the role Amma, our guru, is playing in our life. Our negativities can easily lull us into taking her subtle perfection for granted.

Socrates himself pointed out this danger, noting that often, after he had helped a person make great progress, that person would forget, and sometimes discredit Socrates' role. In their false pride, some began to think, "All this success is due to my own gifts. What did Socrates have to do with it? He did nothing!"

Inevitably, after 'disciples' like this left Socrates and forgot about his grace and the huge role he had played in their unfoldment, they slowly lost all they had gained. Reflecting on this Socrates said, "Neglecting the children I helped them give birth to, they lose them. This is because they begin to put more value on lies and illusions than on the truth."

May we all benefit from Amma's midwifery of paravidya, the highest knowledge, and aparavidya, worldly knowledge, so that we can make spiritual progress and become well-tuned instruments to serve the world.

31—True Worship Means Living Her Qualities

Having received the gift of knowledge through the grace of a true Guru, we are now called to give birth to something within ourselves—the divine qualities latent in our hearts. As Amma's children, we are blessed to have the *Lalita Sahasranama*, the powerful, ancient hymn in praise of the Divine Mother's virtues. In fact, many of us already chant it every day, but chanting the names is not enough. We must try to manifest Devi's virtues in our lives as well. In fact, at the beginning of the *Lalita Sahasranama*, we declare that we will do just this when we chant, *maheśīm aham iti vibhāvaye* (Let me imagine I am Devi).

These words clearly indicate that those who chant the *Lalita Sahasranama* should imagine that they are the Divine Mother, filled with all of her virtues and glories. In truth, we are one with the Divine Mother, but for many of us, it may be too much to believe just yet. So, in the beginning stages, we are encouraged to at least pretend, to "fake it till we make it."

Actually, our archana practice shouldn't end after we chant the last line each morning. The practice of imagining we are Devi should continue throughout the day and express itself in our actions. As Amma's children, we can do this by asking ourselves how Amma would respond when challenges arise in our lives. The prayer, "Devi, let me imagine I am you" is meant to be *lived*. There is no more powerful spiritual practice than this. If we actually live this prayer, transformation is sure to come.

If we want to change ourselves, Amma's grace is always there. This is a fact. So, let us pray for sincerity and dedication in thought, word, and deed that we may share more and more of the Divine Mother's virtues with the world in a spirit of service.

32—Fearless Love

Some years ago, a devotee, let's call him David, traveled to India to visit Amma's ashram for the very first time. When he came out of the Trivandrum Airport, he saw a man standing there with his name, David, neatly typed on a placard. He waved to the man, acknowledging that he was 'David,' and walked towards him.

Out of nowhere another man appeared with a flower garland and placed it around David's neck. They ushered him into an expensive car and whisked him away. Once in the car, they gave him fresh coconut water and snacks. All the while the driver kept asking him over and over, "Sir, do you need anything... Are you too hot? Too cold? Can I pull over and get you a chai?"

Completely exhausted, David fell asleep. The next thing he knew, the driver was opening the door for him. He was expecting to see Amma's ashram, but instead a five-star hotel appeared before his eyes. A welcoming committee was on hand to greet him, but when they saw David emerge from the car, they didn't look welcoming at all. It turned out that he was not the David they were expecting to see.

The committee took back their flower garland and the snacks David had not yet eaten. The hotel didn't leave him stranded though. They called a regular taxi for him, one that he would have to pay for himself. When David arrived at the ashram a few hours later, those on hand had a big laugh about the mix-up.

This story perfectly demonstrates the kind of love we receive from the world, love based on expectations. Some of those expectations are gross. Some are more subtle. But if those expectations are not met, God help you. If the David you get isn't the David you expected, the so-called 'love' stops instantly.

Amma, in stark contrast, loves without any expectations at all. How is this possible? I would say her selfless love springs from her inner independence. Amma doesn't need anything from anyone to be content, happy, or at peace. Her joy arises from within, or as the scriptures say, *ātmānyeva ātmā tuṣṭaḥ* (in herself and of herself alone). This is what allows Amma to be totally loving, free, and fearless. Because she has nothing to gain or lose, she is free of all expectations toward others.

Now, we may think, "How can you say Amma is independent? How could she hold her programs without all the people who help her, like the darshan line assistants, token givers, line monitors, swami translators, and swami musicians? I would respond that even during her programs, Amma is totally independent. If we weren't there to do our seva, any one of a hundred people would be eager to take our spot. And even if they didn't, Amma would still find a way to get things done.

But outer independence is not what I'm really trying to get at. I'm talking about inner independence rooted in unshakable contentment, fullness, completeness, peace, and happiness. This is the independence that enables Amma to love all selflessly.

Amma never confuses her inner contentment with her outer goals. For Amma, these two are like oil and water; they never mix. Her inner contentment remains absolute no matter what is going on outside. As for us, our inner contentment and the fulfillment of our outer goals have become completely intertwined, blurred, and muddied. Spirituality invites us to separate these two aspects, to make sure that our inner contentment never depends on the things we want to accomplish.

Until we understand what true independence is, we will always be frustrated in spiritual life. When moving in society, working with others, and doing our seva, total independence is impossible for us. We must work with others. As Amma says, we are all connected like links of a chain. We should understand and accept this. But when it comes to contentment, peace, and happiness, we must become independent within. Only then will we be truly free and able to love and share fearlessly.

33—Give With a Selfless Heart

Since Vedic times, charity and selfless giving have been a central part of Indian culture. Its importance is stressed again and again in scriptures like the Upanishads and the *Bhagavad Gita*. In a famous section in the *Taittiriya Upanishad*, we are told:

śraddhayā deyam| aśraddhayā'deyam | śriyā deyam | hriyā deyam | bhiyā deyam | saṁvidyā deyam | (1.11.3)

What is to be given should be given with faith. It should not be given without faith. It should be given in abundance. It should be given with modesty. It should be given with awe-filled reverence. It should be given in a friendly manner.

When we develop a giving attitude two things begin to happen: Our minds begin to expand, and renunciation begins to arise. Expansiveness of mind is crucial, for the very goal of spirituality is to understand the inherent oneness and unity behind creation. Giving helps us rewire our minds and leads us from thoughts of division to thoughts of unity.

This attitude is not easy to cultivate; it takes patience and awareness. If we are not aware, we will easily fall prey to the tricks of our mind. We may even think we have been giving when we've only been taking more and more for ourselves.

Once a mother was preparing pancakes for her sons James, five, and Andrew, three. As the boys began arguing over who would get the first pancake, their mother saw a golden opportunity to teach a moral lesson. She said, "If Jesus were sitting here, what would he say? He would say, 'Let my brother have the first pancake. I can wait.'"

James thought for a second, then turned to his younger brother and said, "Okay, Drew, I'll let you be Jesus today!"

As this story illustrates, the mind can be tricky. This is why, as Amma's children, when we see someone in need, we should act without missing a beat. If we delay, we may find excuses not to help. Opportunities to serve should be seen as a rare gift, a stroke of good fortune. If we make a sincere effort to live this way, we will soon find our hearts opening in a spirit of fraternity and harmony toward the world around us.

Once, as a brahmachari was walking through the ashram, he noticed an elderly couple struggling with two large suitcases and heavy backpacks. For whatever reason, he didn't stop to help them and just continued on his way. When he walked back a few minutes later, he saw another person helping them with their bags. He immediately realized that he had missed a precious opportunity to serve.

So, let's remain alert and try not to miss opportunities like this when they come our way.

The second benefit of giving is that it awakens renunciation. Now, don't be afraid. This doesn't mean you have to leave your home, put on ochre-colored robes, and become a monk. That's not what I'm talking about. What we truly need to develop is an *inner* spirit of renunciation. That's why the following Vedic verse was chosen as the ashram's *mula mantra*, its guiding spiritual principle: *tyāgenaike amṛtatvam ānaṣuḥ* (Through renunciation alone is immortality gained).

Rest assured, external monkhood is not essential to reach the goal. In fact, the scriptures are full of stories about householders, like King Janaka, who attained enlightenment. But whether you are married or monastic, inner tyaga, the understanding that nothing is really mine, must be embraced.

At this point you may well be asking, "Why—why is renunciation so important?" It is because any time we claim that something is ours, we are reinforcing false beliefs about who we are. The scriptures say our true nature is *sat-cit-ananda* (existence, consciousness, and bliss). Can consciousness own anything? No, consciousness is simply the witness, the observer.

It is only when we identify with the body, mind, and ego that we begin to see things as ours: *my* house, *my* job, *my* wife, *my* money, *my* children, *my* country. This kind of thinking is rooted in ignorance. And, while we are free to think like this for as long as we want, each time we do, we should be aware that we are distancing ourselves from our true nature—from the fullness, completeness, and perfection we've been seeking all our lives. Each time we believe something is ours, we are limiting creation and denying the whole. Is this not true? Perhaps this is why the scriptures stress giving so much. Giving is a steppingstone that moves us toward the supreme Truth.

In ancient times, people's minds were more expansive. Faith in spiritual truths ran so deep that giving itself became the bank. There was no need for organized banking: everyone simply helped each other. They all understood that "If I give to those in need today, the universe will take care of me tomorrow. If I have knowledge, I give it. Then when I need knowledge, I will receive it. If I have food, I share it. Then when I am hungry, food will be given to me." This was how society worked. The law of *karma*, found in our scriptures, confirms the wisdom of this way of living.

But in today's world we often see good, generous people suffering, while stingy, wicked people thrive. This can make us doubt the truth of the scriptures and the law of karma. But Amma tells us not to worry because the universe is the best bookkeeper ever created. It will make sure everyone gets their due. The scriptures go on to say that if you give to the Guru, you will receive one-hundred times more in return. This is something I have seen with my own eyes.

In the early days of the ashram, we lived day to day, never quite sure where our next meal would come from. But when we brahmacharis asked Amma about buying rice or other food, she would gently scold us, saying, "As spiritual seekers you should have faith that God will provide."

Back then, since I was the only brahmachari with a driver's license, it was my job to buy the provisions. One day, it took me an especially long time to buy everything on the shopping list. When I finally returned to the ashram, I was exhausted and very hungry. I went straight to the kitchen, but there was no food. I was so irritated! I had been given a long list of things to buy, but food had not been included on the list. When I saw Amma, I couldn't hold my tongue: "Amma, there is no food here! How can we live like this?"

Amma replied, "You're wrong, son. There is food. Go take a bath. By the time you have finished, the food will be ready for you."

"I don't want to take a bath," I replied. "I want to eat now."

But Amma insisted. I had no choice but to give in and stormed off toward the water tank. When I returned ten minutes later, a plate of rice was waiting for me. After I had eaten a few handfuls, I noticed the rice was a mix of several types. Suddenly, I realized what had happened. Amma herself had gone to different neighbors to beg, so I could eat. Such is Amma's boundless compassion.

Thirty years later, the tsunami hit the ashram, and the surrounding villages suffered heavy losses. Many families lost loved ones, and many houses were destroyed. The villagers had no way to earn a living or feed themselves. So Amma fed them. Decades earlier, the villagers had given Amma food for one day, so Amma returned their gift a hundred times over.

Sanatana Dharma has always taught that there are two kinds of giving. One is self-interested, and the other is completely selfless. When we give to others in a self-interested way, we do it to protect ourselves. We give to others now, so that when we are in need in the future, we will have the merit of good karma to rescue us.

Selfless giving, on the other hand, is what we see in enlightened masters like Amma. In this kind of giving, the giver sees their inherent oneness with others and automatically helps those in need. Amma never gives with a self-interested mind. She gives because she completely identifies with others' pain and sorrow, seeing them as her own self. She can endlessly give because she is far beyond the body and mind where lack, need, and desire dwell.

Of course, we are not at Amma's level yet, so it's best to just start where we are. Even if we're giving with the hope that we'll be taken care of when the time comes, that's a beginning. Eventually, we'll progress to the selfless giving we see in enlightened masters like Amma. There's a sweetness in giving, in sharing what we have from the heart. And the more we give, the more we'll grow.

When we give with an open heart, we receive both materially and spiritually. More importantly, something within us begins to shift. Our minds open up, and we slowly start to embody the noble ideals of universal oneness and inner renunciation. It's at this point that we truly begin to inspire those around us.

34—The Supreme Role Model

The more we give and serve, the more we are drawn to live with integrity and purpose. But how do we learn to embody these qualities? Most of us need role models who live by these values to light our way.

And so, many of us seek guidance from those close to us, like family members, friends, teachers, bosses, and colleagues. Sometimes we get good advice, and sometimes we get not-so-good advice. We are inspired one moment and disappointed the next, and we begin to wonder if truly good role models even exist.

Unfortunately, when we can't find good role models in real life, we often turn to the unreal digital world, places like Facebook and Instagram. At first glance, it can feel like there are endless mentors to inspire us online. Virtually every post shows someone looking successful, wise, attractive, and deeply happy. You might even think, "I thought Lord Krishna was the only one with a perpetual smile, but look, everyone on Facebook is always smiling too!"

When we visit the unreal world online too much, we begin to compare ourselves with others, thinking, "Everyone is so much more successful, happy, and attractive than I am. I am the only one who is failing in life."

But is Facebook real, or is it just another expression of *maya*, the great cosmic delusion?

I recently read an article that pointed out many are becoming miserable because they are comparing their real lives with Facebook and Instagram profiles. The article went on to say that if we want to know how people really feel, we should look at their Google searches rather than their Facebook pages. On Facebook people present themselves the way they want to be seen. But when people are alone, they secretly search Google for advice.

Last year on Facebook, the top responses after the phrase "My husband is" were things like: the best, my best friend, amazing, the greatest, and so cute. But Google searches told a very different story. The top results included: mean, annoying, a jerk, and does not find me attractive.

The point is, if we look to social media for role models, we're likely to be misled. What people share online may look perfect, but it almost never reflects the full truth of their lives.

Now, I know what you're going to say: "Swamiji, Amma also has a Facebook page." And I would have to respond, "Yes, that's true." But Amma is the only one whose Facebook reality is 100% in tune with her real life. She is the only authentic role model I know of. And two of Amma's beautiful qualities that we should all cultivate are service-mindedness and acceptance.

Amma's entire life is dedicated to service. From her darshan to her vast network of humanitarian charities, Amma's entire life has been about serving others. When people see everything Amma is doing, they can hardly believe it. Amma serves like this because she sees everyone and everything as God. No one, not one person, is ordinary to Amma. From her perspective, every person, every thing, every action is filled with the beauty and splendor of God.

A few years ago, someone asked Amma how she can love and serve so tirelessly. Amma said, "For me, there is beauty in everyone. I am always stunned at the beauty I see. In love, there is only beauty."

Seeing us as God personified, Amma serves us. When we take Amma as a role model, we begin to see others as God too and learn to serve them with love. As we align our lives with this understanding, transformation begins to unfold more and more in our lives.

As the following story demonstrates, we are hardwired to imitate our role models. Recently, I saw some devotees looking at a cell phone and laughing. When I walked over, they showed me the picture of a seventy-year-old devotee back when he was in his twenties. They were all bent over laughing because, in the photo, he had no eyebrows. So, I asked the only logical question: "Hey! Where are your eyebrows?"

He replied, "When I was in my twenties, I was a big fan of the rock star David Bowie. In the 1970s, Bowie shaved off his eyebrows. I thought it was cool, so I shaved mine off too."

If being a David Bowie fan can make you shave off your eyebrows, then being an Amma fan should make you want to serve the poor and needy, seeing them as God. As Amma says, "Compassion is not only the end point of spiritual life, but also its beginning."

We may not be naturally loving and compassionate like Amma is yet, but we can still imitate her and act with compassion. As the great scholar-saint Adi Shankaracharya says in his commentary on the *Bhagavad Gita*: "The characteristics of the enlightened masters are presented in the scriptures as spiritual practices for the aspirant."

Despite being constantly engaged in service, Amma serves with no expectations whatsoever. Whatever comes, Amma is ready to accept it—100 percent. Acceptance is vital. If we can cultivate this quality, then we will be at peace, no matter what happens. When we lack acceptance, life is a constant battle where we are tossed back and forth between momentary elation and tough defeats. When we learn to accept, everything calms down, and we can take things in stride.

Do you know about the turtles who went on a picnic? Well, one bright sunny day, ten turtles decided to go on a picnic. They walked for two days to get to the picnic spot, but when they got there, they realized they'd forgotten to bring the mustard and mayonnaise. They were all very disheartened, but there was still hope. One broad-hearted turtle, Pete, volunteered to go back and get the mustard and mayonnaise. But before he left, he said, "Okay. I will get the mustard and mayonnaise, but you must promise me you won't eat the sandwiches before I get back."

All the turtles agreed, and he set off for home.

One day went by, and the turtles patiently waited. Two days went by, and the turtles continued to wait. But on the third day, Sam, overcome with hunger, said, "I just can't wait anymore! Let's just eat the sandwiches without mayonnaise and mustard." With these words, he boldly took a sandwich from the basket and raised it to his mouth.

Suddenly, Pete jumped out from behind a bush where he had been hiding and shouted, "I knew you wouldn't wait!"

This story shows that the qualities of service-mindedness and acceptance should work together, or else we will end up like Pete the turtle. If Pete had integrated Amma's qualities, he would have gone to get the mustard and mayonnaise because he wanted to serve and then would have accepted whatever happened.

For most devotees, service-mindedness is easier to develop than acceptance. We can all serve to some degree, but acceptance is difficult. The good news is, we have a perfect role model. If we stay with it, and watch Amma give darshan, and keep serving, some degree of acceptance will eventually rub off.

Let me share a story of Amma's acceptance to put some wind in our sails. In 1995 Amma delivered an address at the United Nations in New York to honor the UN's 50th anniversary. As Amma was returning home, we saw hundreds of villagers lined up along the main road of the peninsula where the ashram is. The ladies were all dressed in their best saris, oil lamps in hand.

They lovingly threw flowers along Amma's path to honor her and welcome her home.

They were proud that Amma had spoken at the United Nations and were especially proud that Amma had given the first UN address in Malayalam. Seeing their warm welcome, I turned to Amma and said, "Look how proud of you they are!" Amma laughed and said, "Earlier they threw stones, now they are throwing flowers. For Amma, it is all the same." By recalling how closed-minded the villagers were in the early days, Amma was reminding us not to base our peace of mind on the praise or criticism of others.

So, in taking Amma as our role model of service and compassion, we are really learning to give and receive, to serve and accept with open hearts. And as we practice this day by day, our entire personality begins to change.

And yet, while having a role model like Amma is transformative, sometimes we also need direct, personal guidance. In many ways, Amma has devoted her entire life to offering this kind of personal support and direction.

Sometimes people refer to Amma's darshan chair as a throne. I don't know why. It's just a simple wooden chair covered with a cushion and cloth. I have never seen it as a throne; I see it as Amma's 'May I Help You?' desk. Amma has been known to sit at that desk for as long as twenty-two hours straight, receiving one and all: answering questions, clearing doubts, giving everyone whatever help she can.

A mother's nature is to be aware of her children's troubles. Sometimes even in the mundane world, motherly love transcends logic. Amma often tells the story of her own mother, Damayanti Amma, who knew when her youngest son Satish was hungry, even when he was miles away from her.

Amma describes it this way, "When I was a small girl, I would sometimes play in the courtyard while my mother was making coconut chutney at the grinding stone. Suddenly, my mother's breast would start overflowing with milk, and she would call me and say, "Go get Satish, he's crying from hunger."

"When I would arrive home, I would find my little brother awake, crying for milk. There were no baby monitors back then, but because of mother's love for her son, she could sense anything happening to him, even when she was far away." Amma says, "A mobile phone's receptivity depends on its location. In some places, we don't get any reception. But where there is love, there is always full range everywhere."

Someone recently showed me a video that confirms this. In the video, a mother duck is very upset because all her chicks have somehow been washed down a sewer. Seeing the mother duck desperately quacking near a manhole cover, two policemen walked over to see what the problem was. Hearing the tiny chirps of the ducklings down in the sewer, the officers removed the manhole cover and reached down to rescue the ducks.

They pulled out one duck, and it ran to its mother. Then they pulled out another duck, but the mother still didn't budge. The officers didn't see any more ducks, but they didn't give up. One of the officers leaned way down, found yet another duckling, and lifted it to safety. But the mother duck still wouldn't move. She kept quacking and quacking.

Spurred on by the desperate quacking of the mother duck, one of the officers went across the two-lane road to the next manhole. He lifted the cover, and sure enough, there was the last duckling. The officer reached down, scooped it up, and brought it back to its mother. Now that all her ducklings were safe and sound, she waddled off to a nearby lake with all her duck-babies following in a perfect row behind her.

Over the past forty-five years that I have been blessed to spend near Amma, I have come to see that Amma loves just like that mother duck. She will not give up on even one of her children. But she is not just a mother duck — she is the Mother of All. She never forgets any of us, not even for a moment.

My prayer is that we all grow in the light of her love, becoming children rooted in service who can accept whatever comes as God's grace.

35—Knowledge Frees Us

During the corona pandemic, we were all in lockdown, like those poor little ducklings trapped in the sewer. It was a kind of Catch-22. On the one hand, we couldn't go outside because of the restrictions. On the other, we couldn't bear to stay inside because our minds were driving us crazy. We were caught in a strange in-between state, unable to stay and unable to go.

Of all the lockdown stories I heard, this is my favorite: A man, desperate to get outside for some fresh air, approached a local vegetable seller and asked if he could borrow his cart for a few hours. He didn't want to sell vegetables. He just wanted an excuse to escape his house for a bit... But he was out of luck. The man pushing the cart wasn't a vegetable seller at all. He was just another restless soul who had borrowed the cart to get out of *his* house.

During the lockdown, some devotees in Amritapuri felt a bit hemmed in too, which prompted Amma to ask the ashramites, "Who is really in lockdown? Is it your body, or is it your mind?" Amma teaches that the body, by its very nature, is limited. Today it may be in lockdown, tomorrow it may have a broken leg. Next week, it may be struck down by a bus.

During the pandemic, we were suddenly trapped inside our homes. We had to accept that. But, what about our minds? Well, they can and should remain free. This is the essence of spirituality.

And this is why Amma insists that the brahmacharis and brahmacharinis at the ashram follow a strict timetable of discipline. She does this to help them keep "the remote control of their minds in their own hands."

We should be the ones who choose the channels that our minds visit. When we have gained that degree of control, no one can bring us down. Even if we are in jail, our mind will be totally free, enjoying inner bliss.

This reminds me of an incident that took place in the ashram several years ago. There is a boy who lives in Amritapuri with his parents. As a child, he was always laughing and joking, but he was also very restless.

One day, one of the swamis said to him, "I bet you can't sit still and meditate on Amma's form for even five minutes."

The boy playfully accepted the challenge. "No problem," he said with a twinkle in his eye.

He immediately sat in the *padmasana* meditation posture and tightly closed his eyes.

The swami lovingly watched the boy to see if he would talk, fidget, or peek through his tightly squinted eyelids. One minute went by just fine, but around the two-minute mark, the boy started giggling.

"Aha!" said the swami triumphantly. "You are laughing, not meditating!"

The boy, whose eyes were still tightly closed, replied, "Sorry Swamiji, but Amma is telling me jokes."

This boy had found true freedom and was able to enjoy Amma both within and without.

Unlike this boy, we may not have been joyful when we were locked in our houses. But no matter what the outer restriction, the mind must remain free. The mind should always remain under our control: steady, calm, and free.

When we are alive with spiritual knowledge, we can never be locked down. Amma often tells the following story to illustrate this: Once there was a very righteous king. He loved all of his subjects as his very own and protected them like a father. His people loved him very much. In fact, because of his sterling virtues, they worshipped him like a god. His popularity and fame spread in all directions.

The neighboring kings became jealous and plotted to destroy him. Eventually, they bribed the king's minister. With his help, they attacked the righteous king, defeated him, and locked him in a dungeon. The king was denied all special privileges and was treated like any other prisoner. But even there, in his prison cell, the king spent his days happily, without any hint of mental suffering. The enemy kings were totally baffled by this.

One day, one of the evil kings went down into the prison to ask the righteous king this question: "Even though you've lost your power and been thrown in prison, you don't seem to be bothered one bit. Why is that?"

The king answered, "You can defeat me in war, imprison and torture me, but it is up to me to decide whether I am happy or sad. You see, I have gained true knowledge; as a result, so-called hardships are insignificant to me. I know who I am, and I know the nature of the world. Blessed by this knowledge, my mind is completely under my control. You are powerless to change that."

Amma often emphasizes the same truth, saying, "Like any other decision, happiness is also a decision—a firm decision that, whatever happens in life, I will be happy, I will be strong. I am never alone. God is always with me. We should all develop this Self-confidence."

This calls to mind a verse from the *Bhagavad Gita* that we discussed earlier:

uddhared-ātmanātmānaṁ nātmānam-avasādayet |
ātmaiva hyātmano bandhurātmaiva ripūrātmanaḥ ||

One should uplift oneself by oneself; one should not lower oneself. For oneself alone is one's friend and oneself alone is one's enemy. (6.5)

Reflecting on this *sloka* during the pandemic, I realized how true this verse is. Back then, the only way to reach friends was by telephone, and contact with so-called enemies mostly dropped off. Thus, if we were going to be happy, that happiness had to come from within. We had to be our own friend. And if we found that we were suffering in the absence of enemies, then where was that suffering coming from? It was coming from us alone.

When the pandemic first struck, some devotees asked Amma if she had any advice to offer. She suggested they follow the Government's directions, wear masks, observe social distancing, and stay inside.

But to be honest, Amma's satsangs during corona were just the same as before; nothing really changed. This is because Amma's spiritual teachings have been preparing us to control our minds and to choose happiness from the very start. Here are just a few gems that Amma has been repeating virtually every day for years on end:

- "Understand the nature of the world and develop some degree of dispassion."
- "Live like a bird on a dry twig, alert and ready to fly away."
- "The happiness you get from the external world is like the pendulum of a clock. It's not stable. It reaches one zenith and then moves towards the other."
- "Gain control over your mind."
- "Live in the present."
- "Remember, Amma is always with you."

We may have overlooked how precious Amma's teachings are. If we had been putting them into practice over the years, this lockdown would not have been so hard for us. But it is never too late. We can start today.

Simply choose one quote from above and sit with it in silence. Reflect on whether it is true or not in your experience. Then try to integrate it into your life, even in a small way. This kind of honest effort slowly transforms us from within.

When we are creative, positive, and choose to read spiritually uplifting books, when we are patient with our families and take action to help them, we become our own best friend. If we consistently choose to behave this way, whatever the outer circumstances, our minds will remain perfectly free, even if our bodies are not.

36—See The Good in Others

When do we become our own worst enemy? When we let our mind become negative and pessimistic, when we waste hours watching useless movies, when we endlessly scroll through Instagram and TikTok. In those moments, whether the body is in lockdown or not, the mind is. Life is a great adventure. Why waste it staring at a screen?

In fact, when we choose to 'pass time' in this way, we are not passing time — time is passing us. In Sanskrit, the word for time and death is the same. So, when we waste hours, it is not we who are killing time, but time that is killing us. Bhartṛhari conveys this idea powerfully in the *Vairāgya Śatakam*:

bhogā na bhuktā vayam eva bhuktāḥ tapo na taptaṁ vayam eva taptāḥ |
kālo na yāto vayam eva yātās tṛṣṇā na jīrṇā vayam eva jīrṇāḥ ||

Pleasures have not been consumed. We have been consumed by them. Austerities have not been ignited in us. We ourselves have been burnt up. Time has not passed by. We have passed away. Desires have not ceased. We ourselves have ceased.

Sri Adi Sankaracharya expresses the same concept with poetic intensity in the following *stotra*:

āyurnaśyati paśyatāṁ pratidinaṁ yāti kṣayaṁ yauvanaṁ
pratyāyānti gatāḥ punarna divasāḥ kālō jagadbhakṣakaḥ |
lakṣmīstōyataraṅgabhaṅgachapalā vidyuchchalaṁ jīvitaṁ
tasmāttvāṁ śaraṇāgataṁ śaraṇada tvaṁ rakṣa rakṣādhunā ||

Day by day does man come nearer to death; his youth wears away; the day that is gone never returns. Almighty time devours everything; fickle as lightning is the goddess of fortune. O Shiva! O Giver of shelter to those that come to Thee for refuge! Protect me, who have taken refuge at thy feet. (*Śrī Śivāparādha Kṣamāpaṇa*, verse 15)

The days that have gone by will never come back. Every second, our lifespan is slipping away. So, let us not just pass time; let us learn to use it constructively, for our benefit and the benefit of the world.

There may have been times when our patience waned, and we found ourselves reacting rather than responding to life. If so, let's use this lapse as an opportunity to see our limitations and make a commitment to improve. For it is only when we know our limitations that we can start to put in efforts to overcome them.

We may have gone into lockdown thinking we were almost mahatmas, but by the time lockdown was over, we probably realized that we have a long way to go on the journey of refining our minds and developing spiritual qualities. That realization is a gift; it is Amma's grace.

Unless we get a good look in the mirror, it is impossible to properly clean our faces. So, if we reacted negatively in the past, or said things we regret, let us sincerely apologize and ask for forgiveness, taking it as a gift from Amma. She reveals our negativities so that we can put in effort to remove them.

Most importantly, let's not focus so much on each other's defects as on each other's positive qualities. Amma always sees the good side of everyone, and this uplifts them. Even if everyone else is pointing out a person's negativity, Amma will always find something positive to say.

Sometimes when I am standing beside Amma, people come to her to complain about others. Often while they are talking, I think to myself, "He's got a good point. That person *is* very egoistic, and many people have complained about him to me as well. In fact, I've seen him in action myself."

Foolishly, I start thinking that Amma is going to call that person and give him a good dose. But most of the time, Amma just says, "Aw, he's so *pavam* (innocent), and he works so hard." Amma is not ignorant of the real situation; she just chooses to see the good in all.

Trust me, Amma knows very well who is working hard and who is lazy, who is humble and who is egoistic, who is sincere and who is feigning. Even so, Amma's heart always feels oneness with everyone. In the same way that we are patient with ourselves, Amma is extremely patient with everyone.

We should all strive to cultivate some degree of patience with others, especially with our family members. We cannot force others to change. Amma puts this idea beautifully, saying, "We need to awaken from within. If Amma tries to force us to change, it's like trying to force an egg open with the baby bird still inside it. It will only end in destruction. When an egg breaks open from within, however, a new creation emerges."

Amma has been endlessly patient with us. Let us waste no more time, but instead introspect, see where our faults are, and make sincere efforts to improve. The perfect spiritual midwife is here; the time is now. With God's grace may we make the very most of this golden opportunity to uplift ourselves. Let us forget each other's mistakes and live in love and harmony as Amma's darling children.

Glossary

abhaya mudra: sacred hand gesture in which the right palm is held outwards with the fingers pointing up.

arati: circular waving of lights to the deity.

aparavidya: worldly knowledge.

archana: chanting of divine names.

atma: the pure consciousness beyond the body, mind, and intellect.

atma jnani: a knower of the Self.

brahmachari/brahmacharini: novice disciple under a guru, following a monastic way of life.

bhajans: spiritual/devotional singing.

darshan: audience with a holy person; a vision of the divine.

dharma: spiritual duty.

dhoti: cloth covering the lower body.

jivatman: individual soul.

jnana: knowledge; direct wisdom of the Self.

karma: action; mental, verbal, and physical activity; chain of effects produced by our actions.

leela: the detached actions of a mahatma, which are conducted in the awareness that all names and forms are superimpositions upon the reality.

mahatma: great soul.

mala: impurities such as selfish desires, anger, greed, and jealousy.

mananam: deeply reflecting on spiritual teachings and overcoming all doubts.

mantra japa: repeated chanting of a mantra.

maya: cosmic delusion.

mudra: sacred hand gesture.

nididhyasanam: mentally dwelling in the essential teaching of Advaita Vedanta once it has been fully understood in order to remove habitual ignorant thinking.

padmasana: lotus meditation posture.

paramatman: supreme soul; the Self.

paravidya: supreme Self-knowledge.

pradakshina: circumambulation of a deity.

prakriti: nature; primal matter; self-centered behavior.

prarabdha karma: the results of actions performed in our past lives; the cause of one's birth and experiences in this lifetime.

prasad: blessed offering or gift from a holy person or temple often in the form of food.

prema: divine love.

sadhana: spiritual practices.

sama-darshanam: equal vision.

samskara: spiritual culture and values; imprints or impressions left on the mind from past experiences, actions, and thoughts (in this or in previous births).

samskriti: cultured conduct; behavior grounded in human values.

sanatana dharma: the eternal way of life; the original and traditional name of Hinduism.

sat: pure truth, pure existence, pure reality, pure being.

satchidananda: existence-consciousness-bliss.

satguru: Self-realized spiritual master.

satsang: spiritual talk; the company of spiritual seekers.

seva: selfless service.

sravanam: listening to the teachings of enlightened sages.

swami/swamini: male and female monastic, respectively.

tabla: pair of Indian hand drums.

tyaga: renunciation; self-sacrifice; inner letting go.

unniyappam: traditional Kerala sweet.

varada mudra: a sacred hand gesture in which the left palm is held outwards with the fingers pointing down.

vikriti: selfish behavior that deviates from dharma.

yajna: sacred acts of worship offerings to the Divine; acts of selflessness.

yoga: union.

yuktah: unity.

www.ingramcontent.com/pod-product-compliance
Lightning Source LLC
LaVergne TN
LVHW051736080426
835511LV00018B/3102